TACTICAL
PIKE FISHING

TACTICAL
PIKE FISHING

Mike Ladle and Jerome Masters

The Crowood Press

First published in 2009 by
The Crowood Press Ltd
Ramsbury, Marlborough
Wiltshire SN8 2HR

www.crowood.com

British Library Cataloguing-in-Publication Data
A catalogue record for this book is available from the British Library.

ISBN 978 1 84797 139 5

Acknowledgements
We are grateful to all the friends and colleagues who have been involved
in both our research and fishing activities over the years. Particular
thanks are due to our fishing pals Nigel Bevis, Stuart Clough, Richard
Gardiner, Ben Ladle, Richard Ladle and Ben Lagden. In addition,
John Armstrong, Bill Beaumont, Rudi Gozlan, Anne Magurran, Neasa
McDonnell, Adrian Pinder, Luke Scott, Neil Trudgill and Stewart
Welton have been generous with pictures and advice. We would also
like to thank the Freshwater Biological Association, The Centre for
Ecology and Hydrology and The Environment Agency for their support
during our employment as ecologists. Jerome's PhD studies were
funded by a Freshwater Biological Association Frost Scholarship.

Dedication
This book is dedicated to Lilian and Vicky

Typeset by Servis Filmsetting Ltd, Stockport, Cheshire

Printed and bound in India by Replika Press Pvt Ltd

CONTENTS

INTRODUCTION

This book is not written specifically for the 'specimen hunter' whose only objective is to catch the biggest pike that swims (although it might help to do just that). In practice there are very few waters (these are generally reservoirs full of stocked trout as it happens) containing sufficient 'monsters' to make this more than a pipe dream for most of us. *Tactical Pike Fishing* is for the angler who, like the authors, simply wants the frequent, heart-stopping pleasure of seeing that flash of green lightning as a fish lunges from cover to take the lure or bait.

The text is in two parts. The first nine chapters cover what's known about the amazing habits of the pike that can help us to discover, where, when and how to bring more and bigger fish to the net. We explain how recently science, and particularly the use of radio-tracking technology, has cleared up some of the questions to which all pike anglers would like the answers.

The second part of the book consists mainly of personal piking tales and the excitement, enjoyment and occasional disappointment that is pike fishing. To make it easy to pick out facts that might improve catches, these are listed periodically in 'fact boxes'.

Few anglers can have tried every conceivable approach to catching pike and we are no exceptions. Static legered dead baits, successful and popular though they are, do not play much of a part in our piking experience. We have caught a few in this way and Mike recalls hooking (and losing) a huge pike in the process of trying to catch eels on dead fish, but we are certainly aware of our deficiencies in this area. Similarly we are not well versed in the modern cult of catching pike on the fly. However, we have done a fair bit of fly fishing and caught numbers of pike on flies intended for trout or salmon, so we appreciate the excitement engendered by a well bowed rod and a whirling, buzzing fly reel. Our friend Dr Stuart Clough has caught some good pike on the fly and has kindly helped to fill in the gap. Despite the above limitations, the accounts of fish lured on artificials, wobbled dead baits and live baits provide enough scope for new and exciting approaches to satisfy even our own demanding enthusiasm.

Most of our piking has been carried out on the rivers where we did our own research. This is both a weakness (due to the limited range) and a strength (because we have an in-depth understanding of our own waters). Nevertheless, over the years we have fished lakes, ponds, canals, rivers and streams throughout the UK. Despite the fact that every water is different in character and may therefore need a special approach, we are confident that 'a pike is a pike', wherever it happens to be lurking. In other words the methods outlined in these pages can successfully be applied anywhere in the world that *Esox lucius* plies its trade.

1 CHOOSING A PITCH

Where should you put your bait or cast your lure? To gain the upper hand on its victims and to save energy during the (sometimes long) wait for a suitable meal, the pike must choose its haunts carefully – so should you!

An Ideal Scenario

Grey wisps of mist are rising from the surface of the river as you make your way through the dewy grass. The water is almost bank-high, backed up by the accumulated weed growth of the summer, but it is gin-clear. The sun will soon be up and the pale blue sky, with just a few white clouds, suggests that it is going to be a hot day – not ideal for piking – so now's the time of day to catch a fish if you are going to.

Just in front of you is a small weedy bay. There is one obvious, V-shaped gap in the waxy leaves of pondweed that cover the surface of the water. The wide end of the V faces the open water of

Pike 'lies' in still water. Overhead cover of lilies or bushes and bankside reeds will all hold pike.

Pike 'lies' in a river. The pike often lie in slacks with weed cover where they have access to prey fish in the flowing water.

the river, which glides steadily past. This, you think, is the perfect spot for a pike. Lying quietly in the almost still water, shaded by the floating leaves and camouflaged by the dappled light falling through the pondweed stems, the fish looks out of its hidey hole, senses alert, towards the brightly lit, clear flowing water of the river where the dace and grayling swim.

You lip-hook (through both lips) a 15cm dace dead bait on your single circle hook with the barb flattened just enough to stop the bait slipping off. You slide a little cork, slit with a razor blade to make it grip tightly, onto the line just above the wire trace so that the bait can't sink deeper than half a metre and swing your offering into the 'pike's doorway'. Of course you can't be sure that a pike is currently in residence, but you've chosen a spot with all the best habitat features.

Over the next minute the cork and its suspended bait does a slow circuit of the open

water at the mouth of the weedy V. Nothing happens. Perhaps the pike is elsewhere. Perhaps it is simply 'looking the other way'; if this is the case it will have to make a slow turn and line itself up before striking (any sudden movement could alert its potential victim). You lift the rod and twitch the cork along the top. It makes a loud pop and a few bubbles; under the glassy surface you see the dead bait rise sharply in the water and then wobble slowly downwards. Even though it is what you are hoping for, you are still totally shocked by a sudden swirl and a lean green flash. The cork shoots away into the open water and then slowly moves back towards you beneath the surface. You tighten the line and feel the weight of the fish for the first time. A couple of taps on the line show that the pike is adjusting the position of its catch. Not wishing to hook the fish deeply (although with a circle hook this hardly ever happens), you tighten the

Playing a river pike. The fish attacked from under the weed mat to the left of the angler. There is another similar mat on the right of the picture.

line and the fish plunges off into the flow with the clutch buzzing sharply.

After a couple of minutes of give and take, in which the fish burrows into a weed bed and has to be extracted by being physically hauled backwards (thank heavens for modern braided lines!), you have your capture, finning gently, just by the bank. You slip the net into the water in the little bay where the pike was lurking and then gently draw the fish towards the meshes and slide it over the rim. It's yours! The hook is just under the edge of the upper jaw so you lean down and slide it free with the forceps. Lowering the net, you allow your pike to swim out and away. It was a nice fish of about ten pounds, but no monster, so there was no point hauling it out of the water for weighing – much better to release it with a minimum of stress. After you've stopped shaking, you tidy up the gear, put on fresh bait

and try to find another 'pikey' spot before the sun is too high in the sky.

Useful Pointers Towards an Ideal Spot

So, how did you know that there was likely to be a pike in that place? Well, these fish are ambush predators, built for making sudden rapid lunges at their prey. A pike has most of its fin area near the back end to maximize the thrust provided by all the white (instant action) muscle. Their bodies are not designed for fighting against strong flows and their stamina is limited. Pike are not great swimmers and, although they can survive in rivers where there are powerful currents, they will normally seek out the slower-flowing pools and backwaters.

Scientific research, in which fish were observed in flow tanks, has shown that pike can

A beautiful pike slides towards the bank. Time to get the net into the water!

Richard Ladle with a modest, but beautifully marked, river pike.

swim for about 50m at a time against flows of up to 1.2m per second (pretty fast running water). Bigger pike are more inclined to swim against such flows than their smaller relatives. Pike will leave slack pools and work their way upstream, provided the inflows are less than about 1m per second. If possible, they will choose resting places where they can hide without expending too much energy and without constantly having to adjust their position. Movement, apart from being tiring, could give away their hiding place to potential prey. There is no problem finding a bit of quiet water in lakes and ponds, but in rivers the fish will try to get out of the main flow. For preference, bays, backwaters and gentle eddies will be the spots to seek pike. However, even small depressions in the riverbed or slacks behind rocks or clumps of weed may suffice and should not be ignored.

Secondly, whether they are in still or flowing water, the fish will seek cover. Ideally they require overhead shading on or near the surface of the water, for example lily pads, floating rafts of debris or the waxy leaves of pondweeds or bistort. Trailing grasses, submerged roots or low-growing, overhanging bankside vegetation are also suitable lairs. From the pike's point of view, this type of cover allows them to *see without being seen*. The principle is exactly the same as a person standing in a dark room and looking out into a well-lit street; it is much easier for them to see the approaching door-to-door salesman than vice versa. It has been suggested by scientists that the pike may (like a good photographer) *even prefer to have the sun behind them* and that they might shift positions at different times of the day to achieve this.

Thirdly, pike employ camouflage. The counter-shaded body, dark on top and lighter underneath, tends to merge into the background with the light falling on it mainly from above. The dappled gold and green flanks blend into the green weedy surroundings and also match the spots and streaks of light that pierce the overhead cover. Little pike tend to have more golden streaks than spots; this may be

Our pal Ben Lagden playing a pike that was lurking in the shade of the big bush on the river bank.

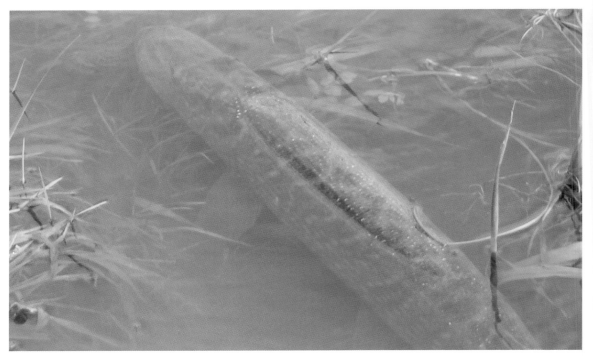

The network of pale lines on a green background provides perfect camouflage for a pike lurking under weeds.

Baby pike like this tend to have golden streaks on their flanks.

By the time the fish have entered their second year the streaks have broken up into a pattern of spots.

something to do with them spending more time in dense weed growth. The patterns of spots on large pike are more or less fixed and individual fish can be recognized by them. The fish squeeze the very last benefit from their hiding capability by having a rounded body cross-section and by leaning slightly to one side so that, seen from the front, they do not (like most fish) hang symmetrically in the water. These two features make them look very 'unfishlike' and 'unpredatorlike' when seen from dead ahead (the dangerous view).

All of these habitat characteristics, shelter from flow, overhead shading and the ability of the fish to merge into a weedy background are useless unless the pike is near a suitable food supply, so the fourth thing to look for will be the availability of *vulnerable* prey. Different prey fish will react in different ways when they are attacked. In general they will either flee or dive for cover. In either case, if they happen to be swimming in open water, they will require an escape route. The pike, on the other hand, needs to catch them in the open but near enough to its hidey-hole for a lightning lunge to reach them before they can escape. The whole thing is a constant game of cat and mouse (or pike and roach if you like), with the prey trying to feed, breed and migrate, etc., without being eaten, and the predator constantly attempting to take the prey unawares.

Scientists have suggested that pike of different size groups choose different places in which to live (this makes sense knowing, as we do, that large pike often eat smaller pike). Tiny pike (less than 15cm long) prefer dense vegetation in areas inaccessible to larger fish. Fish up to 35cm in length still live in pretty thick vegetation but larger pike may also be present. Medium-sized fish (up to about 55cm) are also associated with plants, but these may be less densely growing stands of reeds, lilies or submerged waterweeds. The biggest pike are not quite so keen on vegetation (although experience shows, of course, that they will still use clumps of plants as cover when they are hunting) and may wander freely. Other studies have confirmed that the smallest pike are usually in the areas of densest vegetation. Bear in mind that a thick mat of weed at the water surface may conceal open space beneath and could provide overhead cover for even the biggest fish.

In rivers like the Dorset Frome (where we have done much of our own tracking and fishing), the baby pike may be able to move safely from weed bed to weed bed, becoming widespread throughout the river over their first year of life. Of course, some will be luckier than others and find good feeding spots more or less from the word go. Despite the heavy weed cover, many young fish may be eaten by their relatives before they even get going.

Obviously these facts are just a few clues to the likely whereabouts of pike and the patterns will differ a lot between lakes and rivers or between large and small water bodies, but the general principles are universal.

Where Do Pike Like to Live?

So what sort of place do pike prefer to live in? Jerome carried out some experiments in huge fish tanks (flumes) at the Almondbank unit of the Scottish Fisheries Research Service in Scotland. Young-of-the-year pike were studied in 'landscaped' sections of a very large glass tank to see where they chose to stay, whether

they would be more active during the day than at night, and whether habitats with plenty of cover would be preferred. To reduce variation, all the pike were full brothers and sisters, the offspring of one male and one female caught in Loch Freuchie, Perthshire, in the spring of 2002. After hatching, the pike were kept in plain glass aquaria, under bright light during the day and dim conditions at night. At first the pike were fed on water fleas and, once they became larger, on a diet of earthworms (yes, they do eat them).

The pike were put in four identical sections of a very big glass-sided indoor tank, shrouded in black plastic to avoid them being disturbed. They were identified by PIT tags (tiny identification chips, a bit like the ones on your credit card), which were injected into the fish. The tag is read by means of a 'reader' that displays the unique number of the chip implanted in the fish. The chip does not need any electric current to make it work and the 'readers' can be either hand-held or fixed in the water. Some readers are able to store the numbers of many fish before they are downloaded to a computer. In the past, tag-reading distances have been very short (less than 30cm), but they are being improved all the time so that tagged wild fish, swimming through a suitable counter, can now be identified. Each section of the pike tank was divided into five chambers with detectors that automatically logged when a pike moved between sections. Every chamber had a bed of stones.

The five chambers represented a reed bed; a shallow area with no shelter apart from a short section of drain pipe; a deeper pool with overhanging cover; a second shallow with no cover; and lastly, a shallow with only a few reed stems. The water in the tank was pumped from the nearby River Almond.

Pike have been shown to become inactive after feeding, so the fish were not fed during the time they were held in the tanks. Pike that were waiting to take their turn in the test were fed. Lack of feeding also reduced disturbance to the experimental fish.

Lights were switched on between 06:00 and 07:00 (daylight), and off between 17:00 and 18:00 (darkness). After lights had been switched

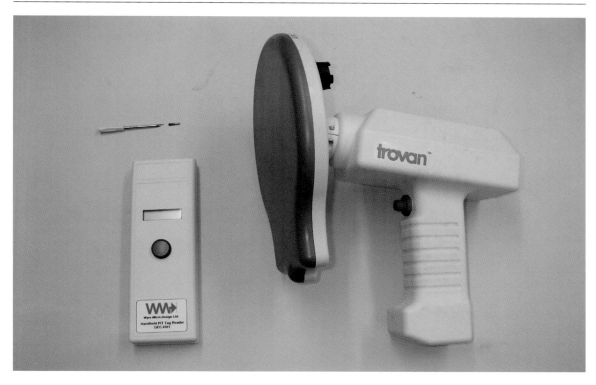

Hand-held PIT tag reader. Using this gadget the 'micro-chip' implanted in the fish reveals its identity.

A small PIT tag that holds a coded number, allowing the fish to be identified if it is scanned closely by an electronic 'reading' device.

A larger PIT tag, which can be used on bigger pike and is readable from a greater distance.

off, sections were often faintly illuminated until sunset.

So what were the results? As expected, the pike were most active in daytime with 82 per cent of movements taking place during the daylight hours. At night the pike seemed to 'sleep', resting on the bed of the channel. The little pike preferred the deepest available water with lots of cover. Nine of the sixteen fish tested chose to live in the deeper pool (still not *very* deep), whereas the other seven opted for artificial reed beds. Open water was generally avoided. Fish living in the pool tended to lie under the area of overhead cover. In fact pike were recorded as being beneath the overhang during 85 per cent of the 239 observations of pike in the pool.

So there we have it. These are the characteristics of a good pike 'lie' (at least for smaller fish but probably for larger ones too) – a slack, shady, shallowish, reedy place, with the widest possible view of well-lit, open water. Of course it should also be populated by lots of suitable prey fish.

Undoubtedly there will be a limited number of such 'good hunting spots' in any lake or river, so not all pike can be in the very best 'lie' at once. In addition pike of different sizes need slightly different places in which to live. As we'll see later, small pike will generally occupy

shallower, weedier spots than their larger kin. These shallow vegetated places are exactly the sort of areas in which the young of many fish species spend most of their time – just what the 'growing' pike needs. Another study has shown that where two *similar-sized* young pike are in the same area, the dominant (larger) one will hog the shallow, weedier 'pitch', while its poor relation will have to opt for the deeper open water.

CHOOSING YOUR SPOT

- Pike will choose resting places where they can hide without expending too much energy and without constantly having to adjust their position.
- They need to see without being seen, and may even prefer to have the sun behind them.
- The smallest pike are usually in the areas of densest vegetation; larger pike tend to wander freely, but will use vegetation as cover when hunting. A slack, shady, shallowish, reedy place, with the widest possible view of well-lit, open water is ideal.
- Their chosen habitat will be populated by lots of suitable prey fish.

2 GETTING TO KNOW YOUR FISH

Seeing pike, or any fish, can be a rare event, so how can we find out what's going on underneath the water?

We should bear in mind that pike are big business! Scientists, fish farmers and anglers are all agreed on that. In recent times there has been a great deal of research into the whys and wherefores surrounding the lives of these fish. Highly detailed and very technical books, such as Dr Craig's *Pike: biology and exploitation*, have been written and big scientific meetings, one in 2004 and a second 'The International Pike Symposium' in 2006 have been held. The latter dealt only with pike, delving into all aspects of the biology and behaviour of these fantastic predators. Much of this material is not readily available to pike anglers and even if we could get hold of it the jargon and obscure language would make it almost impossible to understand. So here we are going to attempt to distil some of the facts from this mass of science and to see whether they are relevant to catching more and bigger pike (as you might guess, some are – some aren't).

the best times and places to catch pike! Or do we? By fishing for pike frequently (and catching a lot of them), it is possible to build up a series of 'snapshots' of pike preferences. Sometimes you will have good days when several fish are caught and on others you won't be able to 'buy a bite'. If you keep careful records of all your fishing trips and the conditions on each occasion, it will be possible, in time, to see patterns in your catches. Certain swims *may* consistently produce big fish in February and March; catches *may* fall off when temperatures are high; bites *may* be more common in the hour after dawn (if you are one of the fortunate few who can rake themselves out of bed at such an hour); and so on.

However, this is a very hit-and-miss approach and it is dogged by the fundamental problem of all fishing. You rarely know whether failure to catch is because the fish are not biting or because they are simply not there. Of course, you can make educated guesses about these options, but in truth you could do with more information. How can you obtain these facts?

The Right Place and the Right Time

Since the main secret of catching any fish is being in the right place at the right time, 'Location! Location! Location!' is of most interest to anglers. As it happens, scientists from all over the world have studied the habitats favoured by pike, mostly in still waters, by monitoring catches, by watching the fish, by snorkelling and scuba diving, by mark-recapture methods and by radio and acoustic tracking.

Of course, as pike anglers we all know exactly

The Scientific Approach

Just how do scientists find out about pike and their activities? The simple approach is what any good angler does instinctively, that is to spend lots of time watching the fish. Unfortunately this only works when the light is good, the water is clear and the fish are near the surface. Pike will often 'bask' and it is certainly possible to see them doing this. Careful observation over a period of time may give clues to the areas that contain the most or biggest pike.

However, if you want to find out more about what the pike are doing when you cannot see them, more subtle approaches are required. By logging where the fish are caught, either on rod and line, in nets, in traps or by electric-fishing tactics, it may be possible to build up a more detailed picture of the places that pike prefer.

By far the best way to find out what's going on down there would be to attach tags to a few pike and then to follow them about. However, in all honesty radio tags and the gear needed to track them would be far too expensive for us anglers to use, even if we had the expertise and could obtain the necessary licences to do the work. Fortunately, however, scientists do the job for us and although they may not necessarily be interested in catching pike, the information they publish can be invaluable to the pike angler.

Having spent many years radio tracking and observing pike in rivers as part of our jobs, we can now make this information available to all pike anglers. The principle is very simple. You attach a little radio transmitter to the fish and, by using a directional receiver (similar to a television aerial – it has to point in the right direction to pick up a good signal), you can pinpoint the pike's whereabouts. If you do this to several fish in the same water it should be possible to see if there are any patterns in their movements related to the time of year, weather, time of day and so on. Of course, this is just what the keen pike angler wants.

I suppose these days everyone has seen pictures of seals with radio transmitters glued to their heads or elephants wearing huge radio collars round their necks. However, when it comes to tracking fish it's not so easy and it is only quite recently that improvements in technology have made it possible to attach small, streamlined, waterproof tags to the outside of (say) a dace or to insert smooth, bullet-shaped tags into the body cavities (pike) or down the throats (salmon) of larger fish.

Of course, to tag a fish it must first be caught and quietened down with anaesthetic before being subjected to a minor surgical operation. After tagging, the fish is then put in a large tank of fresh, clean water until it gets over its experience. The whole process from catching to recovery probably takes only about five minutes, but when we return the pike to the lake or river, the first question is, will it behave normally? There's little point in tracking a fish that simply feels so under the weather after its spell on the 'operating table' that it won't co-operate. Fishery scientists, perhaps even more than anglers, really do want their released fish to behave in a 'natural fashion' so they take great pains to minimize the effects of tagging on the fish. Firstly the tag must be only a tiny percentage (say not much more than 1 per cent) of the weight of the fish. It is interesting that when we tag small fish like dace, at first they often 'lean' towards the side with the tag as they are recovering from the anaesthetic but they quickly regain their balance.

So, the tags, each containing a tiny transmitter and a battery, are fitted to the fish. For small species, such as dace, this is done with a little external harness made of the same material as the 'dissolving thread' used to stitch wounds in hospitals (the idea being that the tag falls off when the battery has run down). Alternatively the tag may be placed inside a larger fish (pike, for example) following a tiny surgical operation. While it sounds a bit gruesome, this is generally better for the fish than using an external harness. Internal tags will not cause any extra drag when the fish swims, nor will the sutures be pulled by the tag, which can potentially cause infection.

Each tag has a special frequency so the pike can be individually identified. It is often possible to determine where a particular fish is situated to within a metre or less, even in the dirtiest water or the gloomiest conditions.

Some more sophisticated tags that we have used for pike incorporate an 'activity' switch which gives off a different signal when the fish accelerates suddenly (for example, strikes at prey or is given a sudden scare). By 'listening' for these 'movement' signals it is possible to tell when a pike is actively feeding. A good deal of the scientific information in this book has been obtained using such methods. To test whether the 'activity tags' would respond to sudden acceleration of a feeding pike, they were first waved about inside plastic lemonade bottles filled with wet, sloppy spaghetti (the nearest simulation we could find to the soft, moist internal organs of a real pike).

Electric-fishing from a rubber boat is a skilled and tricky business.

Electric-fishing small streams can be labour-intensive.

Pike Alice being stitched up after tag insertion.

Pike Quentin recovered after being fitted with a tag and ready to go back into the river.

Trying to locate a radio tagged pike with tracking equipment.

Logging data into a laptop computer on the river bank.

Quite often, as an angler, you can catch the same pike more than once. Sometimes the fish will be recaptured in exactly the same spot as before and you may assume that these fish don't move about much. As it turns out you would be quite wrong!

Much effort has been put into finding out whether pike stay put or move about a bit. For example, in one study, pike that were tagged in lakes mostly stayed within about 100m of where they had first been caught. It's possible that they feel safer where they know the surroundings and particularly where they are familiar with neighbouring pike. When food is a bit scarce, the advantages of familiarity with both location and fellow predators means that pike are frequently prepared to stay put until things look up.

GETTING TO KNOW PIKE'S HABITS

- It's hard to know whether failure to catch is because the fish are not biting or because they are simply not there.
- Logging catches may help us to build up a more detailed picture of the places that pike prefer.
- It's likely that pike feel safer where they 'know' the surroundings and particularly where they are familiar with neighbouring pike.

3 WHAT PIKE LIKE!

So what has all the science and technology revealed about where to find pike? Not surprisingly, in lakes the abundance of pike is strongly linked to the amount of waterweed. In a nutshell: fewer weeds equals fewer pike. It almost goes without saying that young pike need different living conditions to older fish and there's often a gradual shift in these requirements as they grow. These changes happen particularly quickly in the first year of life. By counting baby pike, using traps or electric-fishing, it has been shown that the tiny fish prefer water of less than half a metre in depth. The preferred depth increases to something like 1.5 or 2m by the time they reach a year old. Depth seems to be less important once the fish get bigger. In rivers, young pike that stay in places such as shallow drainage channels often fail to find enough fish to eat and grow more slowly than their brothers and sisters that move out into the main river where potential prey are usually much more plentiful.

Pike don't like warm water, but young pike in their first year are a bit more tolerant than their elders and tend to grow better in water of higher temperature (as high as 26°C) than they do later (when they prefer it to be about 19°C). This is hardly surprising considering the shallow, weedy conditions that the younger fish favour. We can assume that, from the angler's point of view, high water temperatures (above about 20°C) in summer are likely to put pike 'off the feed', at least during the heat of the day. Evening and early morning sessions should be the most productive in these conditions. Temperature-sensing radio tags attached to pike have shown that they are likely to seek cooler conditions if the water gets much above 20°. Growth is reputed to be best at 18°C (not very different to the 19°C mentioned above) and to diminish as the water gets warmer than this.

Male pike are usually smaller than females of similar age and it's possible that this may be due partly to them living in shallower and often warmer water than their potential mates. In the UK our long summer days make for better growth but only the very youngest fish are really tolerant of the low oxygen conditions often found in ditches at this time of the year (warm water holds less dissolved oxygen than cold water). In general pike grow best when oxygen levels are highest, so it's worth bearing in mind that, during the daylight hours, weeds produce oxygen and at night they take it up again. Both effects will have a bearing on the feeding and catching of pike.

Pike on the Move

Of course, the pike don't simply have to 'grin and bear it' when it comes to water that is too warm, too cold or otherwise unsuitable. They can up-anchor and swim off to a better place *if they can find one*. German scientists radio-tagged twenty pike (several died or were eaten by other pike in the course of the study) in a weedy, unfished lake with dense reed beds all around its edge. Perch, eels and catfish were the other predators in the lake. GPS was used to locate each fish precisely and the pike were tracked at three-hour intervals for four days at a stretch. The researchers were particularly interested in what the pike did in very hot weather (July) and under ice cover in the winter (January–February).

When there was open water the fish were tracked from a boat with an electric 'trolling' motor and, interestingly, it was found that even when they were in very shallow water, the pike could be approached to within a couple of metres before they swam off. When the water was deeper the boat could pass directly over the fish without apparently disturbing them. In summer most of the lake (about 60 per cent) was open water and the rest was roughly equal areas of reed beds, sparse weed cover and dense weed beds. In summer the water temperature was almost 22°C and in winter it was less than 3°C.

To cut a long story short, the pike moved about more in summer and they were most active at dawn and dusk in the warm weather – it is believed that in the gloom the pike are able to approach much (three times) closer to their prey before they are detected than in daylight, so this could be one reason for the observed twilight activity. Larger pike tended to be further from the shore and all the fish were further out in summer (although some other research contradicts this). In this case the shift was probably because the pike were seeking out the offshore weed beds, which bulk up in the warmer months and are a feature of this lake. In summer the pike avoided open water and throughout the year they were most often found in stands of reeds (note Jerome's tank observations mentioned earlier).

Weighing a 28.5 pounder caught by Nigel Bevis in failing light, at dusk on a winter's day.

Different pike had their own individual preferences: one fish hardly moved at all, staying in the reed beds all the time; another left the reed beds at dusk and after spending the night in open water, came back to the same patch of reeds in the following morning; a third fish shifted about the lake in the summer and stayed in the reeds in winter. A number of studies have found that the largest pike are often more active than smaller ones.

In Canadian lakes pike seem to move about most in low light conditions except when the lakes are icebound. In other situations, radio-tagging has usually shown them to be most active at dawn and dusk. In the same vein they appear to feed more voraciously on overcast, cloudy days. Presumably murky water will, within limits, encourage them to feed even on bright, sunny days. However, dirty water in prairie lakes was suggested to prevent feeding and as a rule filthy floodwater is neither good for the pike nor the pike angler. Despite all these scientific facts, pike are like all other predatory animals and will (indeed must if they are to survive and thrive) seek out the highest concentrations of prey. If you can find the whereabouts of abundant, vulnerable fish, the pike will not be far away whatever the water conditions.

Lake Studies

Let's have a look at some real examples of where pike live. In Lac Ste. Anne, a very large lake in Alberta, Canada, scientists found that most of the fish stayed close to the shore and only 3 per cent were more than 600m from the margin. In summer over half of the pike were in water less than 1.9m deep and 95 per cent were in water shallower than 4m. In winter the fish moved offshore a bit, but this was probably due to the formation of ice in shallower water.

Another study, this time on Seibert Lake, also showed that the pike were in shallow weedy water in summer. Interestingly, on windy days the fish were a bit further offshore than on calm days. It was suggested that the wind stirred up the shallows and the pike, hunting mainly by sight, moved off to feed in clearer water. Small pike (less than 25cm) were almost always in

amongst weeds and reeds, whereas the larger fish favoured rather more open areas and particularly the outer margins of weed beds. Again very few pike, of any size, were in water deeper than 4m. It was reiterated that small and large pike occupy different habitats – not surprising when you consider the likelihood of cannibalism. Despite the fact that they have no compunction about devouring a cousin, a son, a daughter or a sibling, as many as four pike of similar size have been recorded together, in more or less the same place at the same time, but pike of widely different sizes rarely if ever get together except when they are breeding.

In the Eleven Mile Reservoir, Colorado, USA, three-quarters of the pike were in weedy spots, even though only a third of the Reservoir had weed growth. Once again 75 per cent of the pike were in water shallower than 4m even though most (80 per cent) of the water was deeper than this. Curiously, female pike preferred somewhat deeper more open water than males (of similar size). In a turbid (coloured) lake the pike were more evenly spread, irrespective of depth or weed growth. In very warm climates (where water temperatures climb higher than 30°C) pike may regularly move into deeper, cooler water having higher oxygen concentrations in the summer.

River Studies

River pike have been less studied. In the Dorset River Stour pike caught by electric-fishing were nearly all in the reedy margins, and in the nearby River Frome, a good-sized, chalk-fed river, the fish were rarely away from banks or backwaters. Pike in the Plover River, Wisconsin were also in slow-flowing areas with bank-side cover. In some rivers of Southern France, pike preferred slow flows (less than 0.05m per second – in other words almost still water), and in the Thames, acoustically tagged pike seemed to be 'displaced' by floods.

Of course, *even if* you are familiar with the water you are fishing, *even if* you know all the likely spots for pike to be in, and *even if* you have the best bait you could lay hands on, there are times when you cannot get a bite whatever

Weed cutting must be carried out with care because such operations at the wrong time of year can seriously affect survival of young fish.

The Railway Ditch. Reedy ditches make good spawning areas for pike.

you try. Why should this be? Perhaps the story of 'Isaac' (we name all our experimental pike so it's easier to remember them), one of our tagged pike, will make you feel better.

Isaac had been caught (on rod and line) and radio-tagged. The tag worked very well and for over two years we were able to follow the fish as he went about his business. Each summer Isaac spent his time down in the lower reaches of the river. Occasionally he moved from one pool to the next but on the whole he stayed put. As soon as the big autumn floods started Isaac came 'home'. Despite the filthy, turbulent, torrent, within a couple of days he would be back at his winter quarters *several kilometres upstream* of his summer haunts. Although it must have been difficult for him to see, and even more difficult to swim against, the flow, he would make his way unerringly back to the 'Railway Ditch' where he had been first caught and tagged.

Anyway, after a couple of years it was considered that the batteries of Isaac's tag must be getting a bit low so we decided to try and catch him using rod and line. The idea was to see how much he had grown, what condition he was in and to replace his tag. All in all, we tried five times to catch the fish. We would trek across the fields to the river loaded up with receivers, aerials fishing tackle and tagging gear. We squelched through swampy ditches, scrambled through brambles and, on one occasion, ran (carrying all the gear) to escape a very frisky and determined bull.

The fish would be carefully pinpointed with the tracking equipment and we would set about trying to catch him. Live baits, dead baits and artificials were paraded for his consideration – never a sniff did we have. Isaac seemed to be unimpressed by our efforts. Now we have caught lots of other pike, large and small, tagged and untagged, from the same water using similar tactics so we can only assume that when we tried to catch Isaac he was *not hungry enough* to take our baits or *he could tell that they were not right*. The latter seems unlikely, although it is well known that some pike are more difficult to catch than others. Anyway, the moral of all this is that *not every pike is always catchable*. Of course, you know this already. If they could always be tempted, assuming that you could find the pike, you would have a beano every time you fished. Hopefully, after reading the following pages, the number of blank sessions will diminish.

WHAT THE SCIENTIFIC STUDIES HAVE FOUND

- Fewer weeds equal fewer pike.
- High water temperatures (above about 20°C) in summer are likely to put pike 'off the feed'.
- In general pike grow best when oxygen levels are highest, so bear in mind that, during the daylight hours, weeds produce oxygen.
- Pike move about more in summer and are most active at dawn and dusk in the warm weather
- On windy days, lake pike tend to be a bit further offshore; it's likely that wind stirs up the shallows and the pike, hunting mainly by sight, move off to feed in clearer water.
- Not every pike is always catchable!

4 WHERE TO CATCH A BIG ONE (OR A SMALL ONE)

All pike populations are made up of fish of different ages and sizes. Some waters produce more big pike than others, but why should this be and how can we recognize the best waters?

The pike is what is known as a very 'plastic' species, meaning that they adapt very well to the conditions in an enormous range of lakes, ponds and rivers all around the northern hemisphere. They even do pretty well in the brackish (salty) waters of the Baltic Sea. In fact, in one area of the Baltic there are two distinct groups of pike – one that returns to fresh water to spawn and another that spends its entire life in the salty waters of the sea. All pike are great opportunists, eating almost anything that they can lay their jaws on. However, in any particular water they will adapt to the nature of the available prey and they can be very fussy.

Dace are prime pike food in UK rivers.

Growth Factors

If a pike is to reach its full growth potential and become a 'specimen' fish, it must have plenty to eat at all stages of its life. 'Plenty' means that there will be lots of food fish in the water, they will be of the right kinds and sizes (probably a wide range of both) for the pike to catch them and lastly, the competition from other predators and risk of being eaten itself (particularly by other pike) will not prevent it from feeding when it needs to. In addition the water will not be too dirty nor the flow too strong for the pike to hunt successfully.

The growth of pike is affected by many factors. In laboratory tanks it has been shown that both water temperature and period of daylight (day length) have an influence on pike growth. Of course, the availability of prey is also a key factor. Less well understood are the roles of lake size and water quality. In Finland, pike growth was slower in small lakes than in larger ones. Peaty water also favoured the growth of pike but only in the first two years of life (so not of much direct interest to anglers in search of decent fish). Strangely, in two very acid, fish-less (except for pike) lakes, the young pike (up to four years old) seemed to grow just as well feeding mainly on a diet of insects and hog lice, as did their cousins feeding on fish in other lakes – this *must* be unusual.

Adaptability and Environment

In the St Lawrence River, Canada, there are massive areas of seasonally-drowned riverside reed beds and grasses that have long been used by pike as spawning and nursery areas. As in many other parts of the world, these 'wetlands' are being affected by development and scientists are interested in the likely impact on pike. Pike tagged in these places were generally recaptured (by scientists and by anglers) pretty close to where they were released. Only a few fish moved significant distances. Although it was possible, using genetic DNA analysis, to prove that there were quite different groups of pike spawning in areas not far apart, it was basically just one large interbreeding community. It seems that the pike are pretty flexible in the way that they adapt to constantly varying spawning and nursery conditions.

Pike, like any other group of animals, evolve to make the best possible use of the place in which they are living, be it lakes, ponds, canals or rivers. The basic idea is that, whether it means breeding young and small or waiting until they are old and large, they will always produce as many young pike as possible in the circumstances. However, if they get the chance they will shift to a better spot. A forty-year study on pike in Windermere tried to test this idea. Windermere is a very large lake and has two fairly distinct basins joined by a relatively narrow, shallow area. The idea was to test whether the pike were differently adapted to life in the two basins and whether there was much interchange of fish between the two. As a rule it was found that pike born in the north basin, where prey were less abundant and conditions were harsher, tended to shift towards the easier living in the richer south basin. However, by thinning out the numbers in the north it was possible to make pike migrate in the opposite direction. In other words, the pike were making some sort of choice about the best place to live that was not just based on the richness of the water body.

Pike living in streams and rivers also have to make the best of what is often a 'bad job'. In one study comparing three pike streams, it was found that fish in a larger stream generally grew bigger but there was no basic difference in the way that the pike coped with conditions whatever the stream size. In fact, a lot seemed to depend on the relative size of the prey fish (including smaller pike) that were available for them to eat.

Clearly pike are pretty adaptable creatures, so what makes a lake or river good for these fish? As we've already suggested, ideally the baby pike, in their first year of life, must have access to lots of *little* fish as food, so a pond containing only big carp would not be a happy place for them. A river stuffed with minnows and fish fry, on the other hand, could be ideal for quick growth and high rates of survival. Provided pike spawning conditions were good, the outcome of this might be huge numbers of

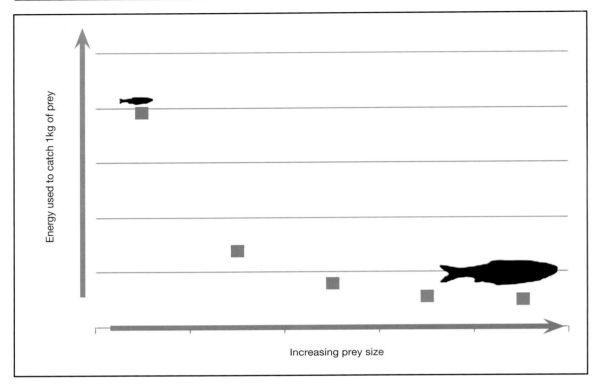

In terms of return-for-effort a pike generally has to work harder to catch smaller prey fish, so (if it can manage them) it will pay to eat big fish.

one-year-old pike all competing for relatively few larger prey fish. As a result, in a river of this type, there may be lots of young, small pike and not many big ones. Of course, places like this are also likely to have a few *very* large pike that have benefited by feeding on their smaller relatives. In contrast, in water with poor spawning conditions and where life for those young pike that did survive was hard (because there wasn't much in the way of suitable food for baby pike), the relatively few 'lucky' survivors may find plenty of bigger fish to eat and quickly grow to a large size.

Of course all these things are relative, so many different types of water are capable of producing 'big' (if not monster) pike. In the UK, we have quite a range of climate (cool in the north and warmer in the south) so that, all things being equal, pike growth is most likely to be slower up in Scotland than in Hampshire or Surrey. This does not mean that Scottish lochs only produce small pike, because in cool conditions the fish usually live much longer and, since they grow throughout their long lives, some of them may eventually achieve tremendous size.

There is also a pattern of water 'richness' in Britain, with the most productive, hardest waters generally being in the south and east of England and the poorest, softest ones being in the north and west (Cornwall, Wales and Scotland). In fact, there is a fairly sharp division between the hard rocks (=soft water) above a line extending from north Yorkshire down to east Devon and the softer, chalk deposits (=hard water) and fertile agricultural lands below this line. This is by no means a 'hard and fast' rule and there are plenty of acid streams running off the gravels of the New Forest in Hampshire, which hold mostly small stunted pike. There are also many very rich, alkaline lakes, in limestone areas of Cheshire and Northumberland for example, where the pike quickly grow big and fat.

Fuel and Energy

A pike is just like any other animal in that if it is to grow and reproduce it must first eat enough food (fish in this case) to make up for the energy it uses in swimming and catching prey. Any surplus goes into increasing the weight and making eggs or sperm. Scientists have tried to make 'energy budgets' for these fish by totting up the amount that they take in and then subtracting the amount that they use up.

The 'lazy' sit-and-wait tactics of pike and the fact that most of their muscle is what we know as 'white muscle' (good for sudden bursts of activity but not much cop for marathon swims) make it fairly easy to work out the energy losses, although these may vary a bit according to living conditions. Pike, as you might expect, are pretty poor 'sustained swimmers' and are unlikely to battle hard for any length of time when hooked. As we've suggested, a fish that is doing nothing but breathing still uses a certain amount of energy to keep its body alive and functioning so, without food, it would gradually fade away. In particular, when the female pike are producing lots of eggs (in late winter–spring), the extra demands must mean that they need to eat more. If the pike has to swim about for any reason its energy demands will rocket. Within limits, all these energy requirements go up fairly dramatically as the water gets warmer, so up to a point the pike will need to eat more in warm water than in cold.

Pike, it seems, are pretty efficient at making use of their prey, they digest and absorb something getting on for 90 per cent of the fish that they swallow. Being so good at feeding, a twenty-pounder (say) will only need to eat about ½lb of food each day to keep it going – weight for weight this is much less than many other species of fish. Of course, a fish of this size will often eat much bigger prey than ½lb, so it will not need to feed every day. This could explain some of those days when there seems to be 'nothing doing'. Radio tracking and heart rate monitoring studies of pike both show that for most of the time they are conserving energy by being lazy. In other words the fish don't do much and this is especially true in the hours of darkness. Of course, it doesn't mean that they will *never* feed at night but it is certainly not the norm for them to do so.

Feeding Patterns

The annual feeding patterns of pike have been studied by scientists. It seems certain that the demands of pike for food vary on a seasonal basis or perhaps there are also much more frequent feeding cycles. Studies in a Canadian lake (where conditions may be quite extreme at times) showed that there could be something like a 100-fold difference between the amount of fish eaten from month to month. Female pike (which again, we've commented, need a lot of energy for egg production) ate about twice as much food as male pike of similar size. Anglers can't fail to have noticed that many of the largest pike are caught in late winter and early spring and these are presumably females fattening themselves up for spawning.

Scientists have shown that pike will often have a feeding spree in the spring when coarse fish prey species are gathered in large numbers at their spawning grounds and (with their attention otherwise occupied on sex) are relatively easy to catch. By mid-summer, as the prey recover from spawning and become fitter, stronger and consequently less easy to make a meal of, the numbers of fish eaten decline (in other words the pike have a much harder time finding food). By the autumn, the baby fish of that year are reaching a decent size so they are worth chasing after and, still being a bit naïve, they make a fairly easy meal for the foraging predators, so the pike again hit the jackpot. It is also thought that the pike should hunt more successfully on some days than on others (according to the opportunities that present themselves for capturing prey), but unfortunately the technology for measuring daily capture success by wild pike is not yet good enough.

More studies in Alberta, Canada, showed that by far the most important prey there, in terms of numbers, was perch, but larger prey species, although scarcer and less often devoured, made a greater contribution to the needs of the predators.

This pike, although it was already digesting a large salmon kelt, managed to take Mike's bait.

The same fish with its 'meal' partly extracted – it seems amazing to us that it managed to engulf such a meal.

The same fish again with the salmon removed. Note how the front end of the prey is well digested already.

An experiment in which pike were presented with rudd of different sizes showed that they ate smaller rudd in preference to big ones. In our view this was almost certainly because under the unnatural conditions of the experiment it was easier for the pike to catch small fish than large ones. In nature, unless small prey is really abundant, larger prey gives a better return for the effort expended. The very variable nature of growth, which is seen between individual pike from the same lake or river, may simply show that some pike are much more skilled at obtaining a decent meal than others.

We've already said that pike grow slower as you go further north; on the other hand, they also live longer – of course, these two things more or less cancel each other out so that, at the end of the day, they tend to reach the same sort of size in many waters. The differences could be due to the fact that growth slows down much more in the cold winters further north. In contrast, in warmer climates, it may be too warm for pike to go about their business of catching prey in the summer months and, together with

low oxygen levels, this could also restrict their growth. Probably factors such as the amount of food available, competition with other pike and the overall richness of the water in which they live are also important.

Growth and Stunting

Pike tend to grow quickly in their early years, but once they reach maturity growth often slows dramatically. In waters where the risk of death (for example, being eaten by something or being caught and killed) is high, pike often mature at a very early age. This is an example of natural selection in action. Pike whose genetic make-up leads them to breed early in life are more likely to produce offspring than fish that leave it later in life as these 'late starters' are more likely to get eaten before discovering the joys of the opposite sex. Over time, the population will come to be made up of fish that have inherited the tendency to breed early. This is evolution's way of trying to compensate for the likelihood of early death and is a widespread strategy in all sorts of animals (and is particularly well-known in fish stocks exploited on an industrial scale, for example North Atlantic cod).

We've all fished ponds in which the perch are stunted – no matter how many you catch, few of them are bigger than 10cm in length. As it happens there are also waters where only small pike seem to exist. Mike fished a canal near Edinburgh where all the pike appeared to be tiny – a fish of a pound seemed to be a good one. The exact reasons for this kind of stunting are uncertain. It may be (as just mentioned) partly genetic, and the pike could have evolved the ability to breed at a small size if they are growing very slowly, but the stunted condition is not always permanent and if the fish are caught and transferred to a richer, more suitable, pond, lake or river they often put on a bit of a spurt in growth and achieve fairly normal sizes.

Perhaps the most likely reason for any fish becoming stunted is overcrowding. This can be caused by very good breeding potential (loads of breeding sites and excellent survival of the baby fish) generating lots of tiny pike. Even in such 'small pike waters' a few fish may outgrow their stunted relatives.

Pike will, in the absence of fish, try to make do with smaller prey such as insects, shrimps and so on. The fish of lakes in very cold climates, such parts of northern Canada, are sometimes more or less wiped out by what is known as 'winterkill'. Where this happens the number of fish available as prey for any surviving pike is drastically reduced. Scientists have copied the effects of 'winterkill' by simply stocking otherwise fishless lakes with pike and seeing what the pike manage to eat and how well they grow for the next two summers. The smallest pike are, it seems, happy to eat almost anything they can get their jaws on, but the bigger ones are fussier and concentrate their efforts on relatively large leeches, which themselves feed on small molluscs or midges. The leeches are often strong swimmers and at times may wriggle actively through the water, making them easy prey for a fish such as a pike.

In this study, the modern scientific techniques used (analysing the pike's bodies for stable isotopes that are known to come from particular food items) showed that the larger pike had switched from their normal fishy diet to one of shrimps, insects, worms and the like. On their impoverished food supply the baby pike grew just as well, at first, as they did in normal lakes containing prey fish, but the larger pike definitely struggled on the 'leech diet'; it's odds on that, in these situations, they would soon become stunted.

It is possible, by using a sort of stomach pump, for fishery biologists to see what captured pike have been eating without killing the fish. Wherever this is done it will probably be found that quite a few of the fish will have empty stomachs. The number with no food in the guts is very variable but we still don't really know why so many of the fish have empty stomachs. Some people think that pike feeding on fish are more likely to feed irregularly and thus will more often have empty bellies than those trying to make ends meet in poor situations by feeding on the less nutritious diets of insects, shrimps and leeches.

Canadian studies also showed that, of those fish that *had* eaten something, most (about 60 per cent) had only eaten one fish, 20 per cent had eaten two and fewer than 10 per cent had managed to catch three prey items. The ones that had eaten several fish had caught them all at about the same time (in other words the fish in the pikes' stomachs were all roughly in the same state of digestion). This ties in perfectly with the idea held by many anglers that pike are a bit like big snakes in that they have a feeding splurge and then spend a long time digesting the food and not feeding (that should make you feel better on a 'blank' day).

So can we sum up the sort of things that could make pike stunted? There are still a few mysteries surrounding 'stunting', but it seems likely that, for young pike (less than three years old), overcrowding and constant struggles with neighbouring fish to obtain food could be part of the story. Perhaps good breeding conditions followed by a deficiency in suitable prey (the right sort and the right size) may be implicated as, in some cases, may warm deoxygenated water in the summer when the fish can find nowhere else to go for respite. Simulation experiments with female pike have suggested that even a quite small (less than 10 per cent) reduction in food, due to competition, could half the size of three-year-olds. Having to eat 'the wrong sort of prey' could reduce size by up to 80 per cent. We've already noted that a good proportion of a pike's diet may come from eating the odd, very large prey fish; if these are absent it can be disaster for the young pike. Warm water *can* cause problems but it has to be very warm. If the pike become stunted in their early years they may grow rather slowly later on. Even in waters where the pike normally grow extremely well, they may die quite young and so do not always reach very large sizes. *Really* big pike are often found in deep, well-aerated lakes with abundant populations of suitable food fish.

Slapton Ley in Devon is an interesting case study of an unmanaged pike lake. It has been studied (and fished) for many years and scientists know a good deal about the changes in numbers of roach, perch and rudd over this time. The pike are less well understood but in the early years The Ley was reputed to have held lots of fish up to 30lb in weight. The baby pike at Slapton feed largely on insects and other invertebrates, but as they get bigger they switch to eating roach and, to a lesser extent, perch. Overcrowding and lack of prey fish (the roach numbers crashed in the 1970s and again in the mid-1980s due to an infestation of tapeworms) are thought to have resulted in the presence (in more recent years) of lots of small pike.

Parasites and Diseases

Talking about parasites, anyone who has kept a cat or a dog will know that these animals are prone to 'worms'. Being flesh-eating carnivores that (given half a chance) feed on the corpses of other animals (rather than biscuits and tinned food), they are particularly susceptible to the attacks of parasites that invade their bodies via the flesh of the things they eat. If your cat is to remain in good health you must worm it every few months by giving it tablets to kill the parasites. Similarly the pike, being a top predator, is also subject to parasitic infestations originating particularly from the animals (fish) that it eats.

Parasites and diseases are very important, not only because they can injure and kill individual fish but also because they may have major influences on the wellbeing of fish stocks (all of us must have heard about the serious diseases that wiped out large numbers of perch and carp in recent years).

Pike are subject to a wide range of infestations, some of which they share with other types of fish and some which are their very own. In various places in the world where pike are reared, caught and eaten (believe us, they are!), their diseases are now well-known. Also, in fish farms and ranches, where lots of fish are crowded together, viruses and bacteria can be a serious problem. However, as with our cats and dogs, worms are probably the most gruesome and important affliction in many situations and their onslaught can debilitate fish and severely reduce their numbers – and more importantly to anglers, their size and condition. All in all, the prevalence of disease is the main reason why we should *never* (however much we enjoy pike fishing and however tempting it may seem to do so) transfer pike, live bait or indeed any other fish from one water to another and why it is a serious offence to do so without having obtained the required consents and health checks.

Anyone who has done much pike fishing will, at times, have landed a pike with unsightly growths on the body; some of these are caused by virus infections. These 'cancers' are usually most obvious in the colder months and often subside in summer. The affected pike will generally continue to feed until they are near death. Pollution may also aggravate these conditions. Pike fry are particularly susceptible to some of the viruses that normally occur in carp, grass carp or tench; in farming conditions, many may die of these diseases. Pike catch lots of other viruses, including a number of the well-known *Herpes* (cold sore) type but, as far as we know, none of them are transmitted to humans (so it's probably quite safe to kiss your 'twenty-pounder' before you return it to the water!). Bacterial diseases (including one which can cause blood poisoning in the fish and is actually called 'pike disease') also occur, as do fungi, including the well-known *Saprolegnia*. Anyone who has tried to keep aquarium fish must have come across this as white, woolly infestations on the skin of their 'pets'. All these infections are more likely to crop up where fish are injured, crowded or stressed in some way.

In addition to the microbes and fungi, pike are attacked by a whole range of protozoa (single-celled creatures), flukes and worms, some of which only occur on or in pike and no other creatures. Flukes often attack a wide range of freshwater fishes and many of them have bizarre life histories, which would make the monster in the *Alien* films seem positively cosy. The simpler kinds are found attached to the outside of the pike or to its gill filaments by means of hooks and suckers. The more complex ones usually live inside the fish and have very involved lives in which they go through a number of stages living in shrimps, insects, snails or pea shells, sometimes moving from one type of small animal to another before being eaten by a fish which, in turn is devoured by the pike. The pike itself is not always the final host and the fluke may only become mature when it gets into some sort of water bird or mammal that eats the pike.

There are also several 'fish tapeworms' that, like the flukes, have complicated life histories; the final stages of some of these are only found in pike. Roundworms, spiny-headed worms and leeches (which may themselves transmit diseases) also attack the poor old pike. All in all, there are dozens of such parasites, so it's no wonder that we occasionally catch a deformed or emaciated fish. Symptoms such as ulcers, discoloured skin, pale gills, swollen bellies, poor condition and general weakness (which may explain why some fish battle harder than others) often pass unnoticed and unremarked by pike anglers. The presence of fish lice and

leeches on the skin of captured fish may be a bit more obvious, but usually these pests cause little trouble to the fish. The removal of pike, which are the final host, from certain lakes has proved to be a successful measure in protecting white fish from one of their main parasites. In Scandinavia and other parts of the world the pike themselves carry a tapeworm that infects carnivorous mammals, including humans – so eating pike sushi or sashimi or indeed pike caviar (yes, it is done) is probably not a good idea.

- To reach its full growth potential, a pike must have plenty to eat at all stages of its life.
- Fish usually live much longer in cool conditions and, since they grow throughout their long lives, some of them may eventually achieve tremendous size.
- When female pike are producing lots of eggs (in late winter–spring), the extra demands must mean that they need to eat more.
- A successful predator will not need to feed every day. This could explain some of those days when there seems to be 'nothing doing'.
- The most likely reason for any fish becoming stunted is overcrowding.
- A small (less than 10 per cent) reduction in food, due to competition, could half the size of three-year-old pike. Having to eat 'the wrong sort of prey' could reduce size by up to 80 per cent.
- Really big pike are often found in deep, well-aerated lakes with abundant populations of suitable food fish.
- Worms are probably the most serious affliction for pike and can severely reduce their numbers, their size and their condition.

5 IT'S A PIKE'S LIFE!

From its beginnings as a tiny, translucent egg to becoming a 30lb killer, the pike is a fascinating creature. Only by fully understanding the needs of the fish is it possible to catch them consistently.

Spawning

As in many other species of fish, male and female pike are almost indistinguishable. Of course, the females are often bigger than the males but there are no major differences in colouration, shape or form to provide a clue to the sex of the fish you have landed. At spawning time, the female fish may be swollen with eggs, and the presence of eggs or milt running from the sexual opening may make it obvious whether the fish is male or female, but at other times it is less easy. In fact, a close inspection will show that female pike have a series of little folds between the two body openings just in front of the anal fin; males show no such folding. Despite these differences, even experts are unable to sex correctly more than about 90 per cent of mature pike in this way.

Pike usually spawn in springtime and they prefer to lay their eggs in areas where there are thick growths of submerged plants (remember what we said about small pike liking thick vegetation). In northern lands pike have been known to spawn in thickets of arctic birch trees submerged by water from the melting snows. Almost as soon as they are shed, the little pale yellow eggs develop a sticky surface layer and become glued to the surrounding stems and leaves.

In fact, pike will attempt to breed almost anywhere that has shallow water and thick plant growth. Grasses, sedges, reeds, water mint, even tree roots, lilies and dead plants, and particularly plants with fine leaves, are all suitable for egg laying. Weedy pools, flooded meadows and ditches and the shallows of lakes and ponds all make suitable locations. Pike don't seem to mind too much whether the vegetation is alive or dead (they will even lay eggs on loose straw bales dumped in the water), but slow flow and protection from disturbance by strong winds also seem to be important for breeding success.

Conservationists have suggested (and made use of) Off River Supplementation Units (ORSUs) on modified rivers where the natural habitat has been altered to serve the needs of industry, navigation and/or flood defence. These ORSUs are simply shallow, weedy ponds dug along the riverbank and joined to the river itself by a channel. They are designed to recreate natural floodplain habitats, such as backwaters and oxbow lakes, which have been lost as people have modified the course of the river. The idea is generally to enhance the stocks of coarse fish, particularly roach and similar species, by giving them a sort of nursery. Of course, these slack areas will also benefit the river's pike population, providing them with weedy margins in which to grow, as well as a ready food source in the form of young prey fish – all part of the natural balance between predator and prey.

From the pike's point of view, waters totally without weeds are a disaster. In such places plastic trellis or fibre matting can be introduced and may act as a (pretty poor) substitute for the spawning fish. It has been shown that well over

Spawning pike in the shallow water of a flooded ditch.

2,000 eggs can be laid on only one square metre of weed growth. Female pike let their eggs go in 'bursts' of up to sixty at a time, moving about between laying the batches. Once laid, the eggs hatch in as little as a week or two (more quickly when the water's warmer).

One thing that stimulates pike spawning seems to be increasing water temperature. Conversely, a cold spell and cooling water may delay spawning activity. In different parts of the wide geographical range of pike, spawning has been recorded at temperatures ranging from under 4°C to as high as 14°C.

Although pike are more or less indifferent to the sort of plants on which they breed, they may have strong preferences for spawning in particular places. In the Dorset River Frome they often spawn in ditches or side channels, although in dry years, when the ditches are too shallow for the fish to enter, the pike will sometimes make the best of a bad job and lay their eggs in the main river. In this river, breeding generally occurs in late March and early April although more recent observations have shown that the spawning season is in fact much longer than this continuing until as late as June in some years. In the nearby River Stour, spawning was observed in April when the water temperatures ranged from 8 to 14°C. Even though the water is pretty cold during the breeding season, pike eggs develop quite quickly and at a temperature of 10°C it would take them only about fifteen days to hatch. At 5°C hatching time would be roughly twice as long. Scientific modelling of a lake pike population by Farrell and others has shown that most recruitment of young fish would be from tributaries rather than from shallow weedy bays. Very few baby pike would emerge from deeper water.

Hatching

After hatching, the tiny 'pikelings' swim up and attach to leaves or weed stems. The newly-hatched pike have a sticky pad on the head that they use to cling to the weeds. Over a period of a few days they begin to swim, returning to the plants for a rest at intervals. After a week or two the swim bladder is inflated with air and the young pike become free-swimming. About nine days after hatching, the yolk is all used up and the little fish must fend for themselves. Even before this, they may catch tiny insects and crustaceans for food. When the pike are only a couple of centimetres (less than an inch) in length, they move out of the *really* dense plant growths where they were born. Of course, this is a good thing to do because the eggs are often laid in drowned vegetation and as the water levels fall there will be an increasing risk of them being left high and dry. Also they need to spread out to find food but even at this stage there may still be several tiny pike in every square metre of water and their main diet will continue to be water fleas and midge larvae of various kinds. These little food animals are most abundant on stands of water weeds. Towards the end of summer, most of the fish move to better oxygenated, open water where there is less plant growth. Why do pike spawn in such 'risky' places? Our guess is that if you spawn somewhere that's just flooded, then there will not be as many predators present to eat your eggs or fry.

On the Frome, we've watched pike spawning in floodwater, in places that have then dried out within days of the eggs being laid. Although we think of pike as being at or near the top of the food chain, baby pike themselves, up to a length of about 10cm, are at risk of being eaten by large predatory insects such as beetle and dragon fly larvae. Mike has seen the larva of a great diving beetle tackling a fully-grown great crested newt, so a tiny pike would be no problem to such a fierce predator. We can speculate that there will be fewer of these fierce insects in areas that have recently flooded, and so by spawning here, losses to predators might be reduced. By laying eggs in short bursts and moving around between each batch, the pike increases its chance of laying at least some of its eggs in a prime spot, balancing its efforts between places with fewer insects and others that will not dry out too soon.

Later in life the little pike gradually shift their diet from invertebrates to fish. In fact most baby pike die in the first few months of life from disease, starvation, and being eaten by beetles, dragonfly larvae, other fish and even their own brothers and sisters. Some young pike hang about on the spawning grounds for months, while others quickly migrate away to different areas. The pike that find the best feeding sites are, by now, growing much faster than those that are 'left behind' in the weed beds and the diet of these 'movers' has at this point shifted to fish. Young pike don't like being kept in tanks without water plants and in these conditions their growth is very variable and much slower than when there's lots of weed. In the River Frome, the fish that 'stayed put' did not gain size and weight anything like as quickly as ones that moved out into the main river. Within a year a fast-growing fish could be as much as 25cm in length.

Survival

The main predators of tiny pike (less than a year old) are in fact the pike born in the previous year. Up to a point, the warmer the summer the quicker the young pike grow and the sooner they are big enough to avoid becoming the next meal for their cannibalistic older brothers and sisters.

It has been reported that, in some European rivers, where conditions are unfavourable for egg laying or as nurseries (because there are virtually no plants), pike populations often have to be maintained by artificial stocking. As waters become cloudier, due to suspended silt or drifting algae, this muck cuts down the penetration of light, the growth of water plants decreases and with the plants go the pike. Despite their ferocious appearance, pike are incredibly sensitive to habitat changes and particularly to the loss of weed growth. In contrast the presence of rotting weeds and/or algae may kill the young pike by starving them of oxygen.

Pike really do love plants. As already mentioned, weeds and grasses are almost essential for spawning and as nursery areas for baby pike. One of the key features in this connection is how young pike avoid becoming meals for their older relatives. Many of the scientific studies on these aspects of pike behaviour have been carried out in quite small ponds by Dutch scientists. It has been found that tiny pike, those less than about 12cm in length, can (and indeed probably prefer to) survive in shallow, weedy spots where larger pike are more or less unable to go. In the backwaters of the Mississippi River there were three times as many young pike in weeds as there were in reed beds and ten times as many as in open water. It is easier for the bigger pike to hunt fish when they are on the margins of the weed beds rather than in the thick of them and this is the sort of place that they prefer to lurk.

As they get bigger, the baby fish must venture (if they are to feed well) into areas where there are even larger pike. In one big experiment where a reed bed was stocked with young fish it was believed that up to 80 per cent of the baby pike could have been devoured by their older relatives. Often, in experiments like this, the method of marking the introduced baby pike (because you need to recognize them when they are recaptured) involves clipping one or both of the pelvic fins, not an ideal tactic as they use these fins for manoeuvring and it may well make the marked pike less agile and more susceptible to being eaten, so it's not easy to make good estimates of how many would survive in nature.

There can be no doubt that, once the young pike leave their densely vegetated hidey-holes, they may be devoured by other pike and it is the smallest ones that will be the most vulnerable. If two young pike of similar size happen to come across each other they will normally lie side by side. However, if one turns and faces head on to the other (and so it seems likely that an attack may be in the offing), the potential victim does a display, arching its body, opening its mouth and flaring its gills in an attempt to threaten and to scare off the potential aggressor. It's also known that hungry pike will rob other pike of their prey if they can. It seems possible that pike living in the same area may get to know each other and while not exactly becoming 'friends' may set up a sort of truce that reduces the chance of them being eaten by their neighbours. Having said that, one of our tagged pike, Nicola, met her end when she was bitten by a larger pike. Poor Nic was found on the river bed, with a tench still clasped in her jaws. We think she and another pike may have been targeting the same fish at the same time, with Nic getting in the way and receiving a fatal bite for her trouble. In another demonstration of their cannibal tendencies, large female pike seem to have no compunction about consuming their potential suitors, particularly towards the back end of spawning time. Talk about 'man eaters'!

Pike tend to become mature when they are about two to four years old (minimum sizes of something like 18 and 26cm in length for males and females respectively) but the sight and/or smell of bigger pike present in the same water can hold them back from becoming adults. Pike have prodigious appetites and if they are crowded together in a pond they may not grow as quickly as when they are thinner on the ground, even if there are plenty of prey fish present for them all to eat.

Population Density

'Just how many pike are present in my river/lake/pond?' is a question that must have occurred to many anglers (particularly after a blank session or two). Well, scientists have spent quite a lot of time and effort trying to find out. They could, of course, ask the anglers but anglers are notorious liars! You only have to stretch your arms apart and everyone, whether they know anything about fishing or not, will immediately recognize you as the caricature of a fibbing fisherman. In order to establish whether angler's reports could be used to estimate the state of fisheries (and so to manage the fish stocks), a study in Alberta, Canada, compared angling returns of zander (walleye) catches with the true situation. In general the anglers more than doubled the number of fish they had actually caught and the poorer the fishing, the more they exaggerated their catches. So what are the alternatives and what controls the numbers of pike in a water?

It can't be over-emphasized how much pike really do depend on water plants or on land plants swamped by rising water levels. Good, suitable, weedy habitats will support a maximum of about one little pike (less than about 10cm long – two to four weeks old), for every one or two square metres of drowned grasses, sedges, rushes or other emergent plants. So the annual 'crop' of baby pike depends largely on the amount of 'drowned' spawning area at the appropriate time of the year. Pike of less than about half a metre in length (what you might regard as 'jacks') are still more or less restricted to fairly weedy areas. It is thought that small rivers and ditches can hold, at most, about one kg (roughly two pounds) of pike for every ten metre square of suitable living space. In big lakes the pike are usually more thinly spread than this.

How were these estimates made? In a few cases ponds have been completely drained and all the fish counted but this is not normally to be recommended. One of the standard methods is what is known as 'mark recapture'. The idea is to catch some pike (say 100) and put them back after marking them (with a coloured dye or some other form of tag) so that you can recognize them if and when they are caught again.

If, at a later date, you fish the same area again and half the pike you catch contain your mark then you can assume that there are about twice as many present (say 200) as you caught and marked the first time. Easy, eh? Lots of things complicate the calculations, but this is the general idea.

In the Dorset Frome, where we did most of our fishing and research, there is on average roughly one pike along every ten metres of bank. Of course, this includes many tiny ones that you would not want (or be able) to catch anyway, but at least it gives some idea of what you are (or are not) catching.

Larger pike are often found in reed beds and the old 'angler's tale' that pike leave reed beds in windy weather may have some truth in it because it is thought that pike will retreat into deeper water if there is strong wave action along the shore. As mentioned already, in Canadian lakes, radio and ultrasonic tracking showed that pike moved further offshore in windy weather (but not into deeper water). They also moved inshore and into shallow water on bright sunny days. Rain seemed to have no effect on the behaviour of the fish.

How Big Can Pike Get?

The pike is essentially a fish of cool waters. Like many other species of fish, the scales and bones reveal their age as rings are formed on them each year. These 'annual rings' usually form in spring, a bit later in old pike than in young ones. Large mature pike also form an extra 'check' mark on the scales at breeding time. When the water is very warm, in summer, the stress may also result in the formation of a false 'check' making the fish seem older than it is. The first scales form on the flanks when the baby pike are just over 3cm long. In fact, it is much easier to read the age of a pike by using one of the gill cover bones, but to do this the pike has, of course, to be killed. In the River Frome, where we did much of our fishing, the pike grew quickest (and presumably were feeding most actively) in the period from May to September.

Female pike generally live longer than males. Not many pike of either sex survive for more than about seven years and less than half of pike waters tend to contain fish much older than this. Only about one tenth of lakes or rivers hold pike that have managed to survive for more than twelve years (the Frome is one such river). Despite these limitations, it's possible that some pike achieve great ages, even up to about thirty years, in large cold lakes.

After hatching, baby pike grow (in reasonable conditions) roughly 1cm every week but there are huge variations and pike of similar age can differ by as much as twice in length and eightfold or more in weight. Given suitable survival conditions, the slowest growing fish often ultimately reach the greatest lengths. Large pike will gain as much as 1.5kg (two or three pounds) a year after they reach about three years of age. They grow best where the competition (other pike) is thin on the ground and where occasional large meals (such as salmon kelts, carp or bream, for example) give them a major boost from time to time.

In small Finnish lakes scientists have found that the pike grow more slowly than in larger bodies of water. They also grow more quickly in peaty lakes than in clear ones. The presence of roach to feed on is a real bonus and tends to boost the growth of young pike but surprisingly if ruffe are present, growth of the predators is slowed down.

So, the growth rate may differ a lot between different waters. Of course, what the pike angler would like to know is how big are the pike in a particular water going to become. In fact, it is possible to calculate how big a pike is likely to grow in the course of its life. For example, in much of North America a probable maximum length is only 83cm, in many parts of Europe pike can reach 112cm, and Asian fish (although they usually grow more slowly) could live a lot longer and have been calculated to achieve the colossal maximum length of 139cm. Female pike are usually almost 8 per cent longer than males of the same age and may finish up as much as 40 per cent longer and almost three times as heavy. In the River Frome females lived longer than males, with some surviving for up to twelve years, while the oldest male recorded was not much more than five. However, one particularly long-lived, radio-tagged male pike (we called him Boris) carried an active tag for almost five years. We think he holds the record for the greatest length of time that a tagged pike was tracked. A testament to the care devoted to tagging and release.

Breeding Grounds

Pike are generally heaviest in the late winter, just before spawning and, as most pike anglers are aware, if you want to catch a really heavy fish this is the time to do it. The fish are known to migrate to their breeding grounds prior to spawning and the male fish generally arrive before the females. This may be because the male fish then wait for the arrival of females and attempt to spawn with more than one partner in succession. In the large lake Windermere, in the English Lake District, the older female fish, of nine or ten years of age, tend to spawn first, with the younger, smaller ones arriving later. In Windermere males, on average, stay for about two weeks on the spawning area while females hang around for only ten days. Pike are known to 'home' to particular spawning areas year after year. Individually tagged pike have been found on the same spawning ground in successive years and one fish came back for at least five years on the trot. There has been a lot of valuable research on Windermere pike by the scientists of the Freshwater Biological Association and it was shown that many fish stay more or less in the area in which they spawn throughout the year but others may move as far as 7km away. The pike in Slapton Ley (Devon) are also believed to spawn in the same part of the lake year after year.

As suggested, it is thought that some pike return to spawn in the places where they were born but it is not known whether this is just chance or whether the fish are actively seeking their places of birth (like salmon). In the Belgian Rivers Ourthe and Ambleve, upstream spawning migrations of 7–8km have been recorded. One tagged fish (known to us as Isaac) in the River Frome, migrated several kilometres back and forth each year between its winter (breeding?) quarters and its summer feeding grounds. The upstream migrations of Isaac, our 'uncatchable'

pike from the previous chapter, seemed to be triggered by floods.

Recent studies have attempted to establish once and for all whether pike, like salmon, actually do return to the areas where they themselves hatched in order to spawn. The novel method used to examine this *homing* activity was to feed a female pike with a fish containing a blue dye. A capsule of the dye was placed inside the body cavity of a suitable dead bait. The dead bait was tied to the end of a line using a short length of sewing thread and the bait was then jiggled in front of a known female pike (located by radio tracking). It rarely took more than a minute or two for the pike to take the bait, break the thread and swallow both fish and dye capsule. The dye migrated through the tissues of the fish to the ovaries where it stained the eggs bright blue. Subsequently the pike was tracked to its spawning ground where it laid its blue stained eggs. The pike fry hatching from the eggs also retained some of the dye and could, for a time, be distinguished from their untagged cousins. Of course, the dye fades so, as soon as they are big enough, the baby blue-marked pike are individually tagged with an electronic 'PIT' tag and then can be identified should they, at some future date, return 'home' at spawning time. We await the results with interest.

Even in waters where breeding conditions are excellent, pike, like other fish, have good and bad survival years. In lakes this may be largely governed by variations in the timing and the amount of rain. This is largely due to the availability of weedy (spawning/nursery) areas at and after spawning time and the risk of cannibalism by older pike. Low rainfall in the winter and spring may mean that there are few places for them to breed. An early 'dry season' can leave eggs or young larvae high and dry. When the weeds die back in the autumn, provided there has been adequate rain and the lake margins have become submerged, the little pike, having spent the summer in lush offshore weed beds, will move inshore again to avoid the depredations of their older relatives. Pike *need* variable water levels and numbers may decline quickly in waters where the level is artificially kept constant.

Typical spawning channel – pike may spawn hundreds of metres from the main river.

Flood conditions. High flows often seem to trigger upstream migration.

Often a strong 'year class' (born in a year when breeding conditions have been good and lots of young pike have survived) will dominate the population for several years after. These strong year classes (large numbers of fish of the same age) can be caused by many factors – absence of predators may be important, as may be (particularly) high water temperature in mid-summer, resulting in better growth and survival of the little fish. More surprising is the fact that high water levels in the autumn, due to wet weather, can have a bad effect on survival. This is probably because high water increases the amount of available habitat and so disperses prey suitable for the growing fish.

THE LIFE OF PIKE

- Pike are sensitive to habitat changes and to the loss of weed growth, but it is easier for bigger pike to hunt on the margins of the weed beds rather than in the thick of them.
- Up to 80 per cent of the baby pike may be devoured by their older relatives, while large female pike might eat their potential suitors, particularly towards the back end of spawning time.
- Hungry pike will sometimes rob other pike of their prey if they can.
- The presence of bigger pike in the same water can hold young fish back from becoming adults.
- In the River Frome, there is roughly one pike along every ten metres of river bank.
- Some pike achieve great ages, even up to about thirty years, in large cold lakes.
- Pike are generally heaviest in the late winter, just before spawning.
- Pike need variable water levels and numbers may decline quickly in waters where the level is artificially kept constant.

6 RED IN TOOTH AND FIN!

Being an ambush predator, the pike must out-perform its prey. Camouflage, super senses, lightning muscle power and deadly fish-trap jaws ensure that *Esox* often comes out on top.

How Do Pike Hunt?

Although pike can locate prey using their senses of smell and taste, and there is evidence that the lateral line 'vibration detectors' may be important for early detection of prey movements, pike feed most effectively in clear water with decent light penetration where they can use their excellent eyesight to locate prey fish.

Pike are often described as ambush or lurking predators, designed to make a fast start and a lightning strike when a prey fish comes within range of their hiding place. They usually take prey from the side and target a position about one third of the distance back from its head. It has been shown that predator strikes on station-ary prey often take place shortly after the fish has stopped swimming (something to be said for stop/start lure fishing then?). They also like their prey to be close before they make a move. Observations on tiger musky (hybrids of pike and its North American 'cousin' the muskel-lunge) showed that small fish strike at a speed of about three body lengths per second. If they miss the prey, they are going so fast and have such poor 'brakes' that they often overshoot it, which means they are in no position to give chase. In fact, pike rarely chase prey after a failed attempt but generally they abort the attack and wait for another chance to strike. This is in contrast to rainbow trout, which can manoeuvre better and will chase after prey that tries to escape.

The Prey

The average size of prey eaten by pike is greater for big pike (even though large pike will still eat small fish) and the favoured size may be a quarter to a third of the body length of the pike. If pike can get hold of prey of this 'ideal' size, they are likely to grow more quickly. Pike not only spend time waiting for and catching food but they then have to hang on to it, turn it and swallow it – all of these activities need time and effort. For example, the pike has to jerk its head from side to side in order to turn the prey fish into a head-first position for swallowing and anyone who has used natural bait must have felt the 'knocks' on the line after a take as the pike manipulated its prey before sliding it down.

Most of the things that fish do – feeding, mating, migrating, etc. – are important in their lives, but one bit of behaviour, dodging preda-tors, is literally a matter of life and death. For this reason a lot of effort goes into camouflag-ing, hiding and beating a hasty retreat when Mr Pike comes on the scene. Any fish that is not very good at spotting and/or avoiding predators will be unlikely to survive long enough to pass on its genes to its children. Of course, on occa-sion, being a quick learner is quite likely to save your skin and scales, so fish are pretty good at changing their behaviour in an appropriate way to reduce the chances of being eaten. Scientists Jen Kelley and Anne Magurran reviewed what is known about the way that fish learn to avoid predators. Since, as pike anglers, we should be trying, all the time, to make our bait or lure look vulnerable, this sort of information is well worth a second look. The first thing to notice is that fish that are familiar with predators often flee faster than fish that have never set eyes on a pike before. Another defensive tactic, used by minnows in particular, is to form shoals and to inspect the pike from a safe distance. In this case fish that are familiar with pike form larger protective shoals. Fish in larger shoals also learn more quickly to inspect predatory pike from the 'blunt end' rather than peering down their throats.

Of course the prey fish are not just there to be eaten by pike and they have many strategies to avoid becoming the next meal. Not all the defence mechanisms are effective all the time or the pike would starve. Sticklebacks, for example, despite being very spiny, are often devoured. Since they are small and relatively slow moving, sticklebacks would seem (apart from their spiky bodies) to be relatively 'easy meat' for a hungry predator. These little fish are known to employ a number of different anti-predator strategies. They may, according to the circumstances, raise their spines, head for cover,

inspect the pike from a safe distance to see if it's in 'feeding' mode, swim away, jump or freeze. No doubt many other species of fish have their own armouries of escape tactics.

Despite the old stories about pike avoiding tench (sometimes known as 'doctor fish') because they are slimy or perch because they are prickly, pike will, given the chance, eat practically any other fish. However, studies in five Swedish lakes have shown that these fierce predators readily get used to feeding on particular species and sizes of prey.

Pike are great opportunists and will switch their diet to whatever species happens to be most abundant and/or most easily captured. Although pike will readily grab and swallow a prickly mouthful such as a perch or a stickleback, they generally seem to prefer soft-finned species, like rudd, as food. However, rudd don't just give themselves up and they are apparently very good at nipping into weed beds when

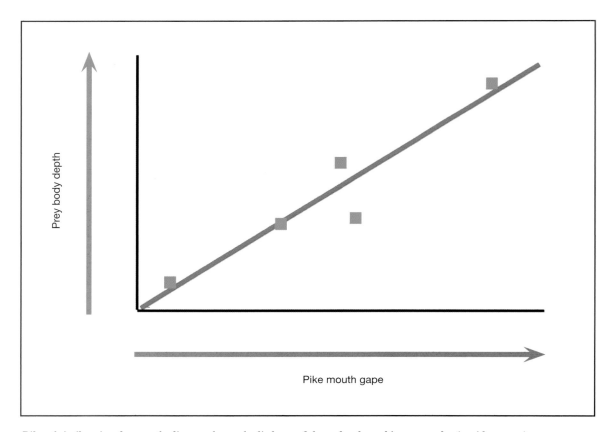

Pike of similar size that are feeding on deeper-bodied prey fish tend to have bigger mouths (=wider gapes).

attacked, so they do much better in weedy lakes than in open water.

In lakes where prey was abundant, the pike were prepared to eat fish of more or less any size, while in lakes with low fish densities only the larger prey, which presumably provide a better return for the effort of catching them, were generally eaten. In fact, in lakes where food was really hard to come by, not only did the pike tend to go for larger fish, but they actually had bigger mouths (=wider gapes) so that they could deal with these more awkward food items. It's interesting to consider that fish, such as anglerfish, living in the deep oceans where food comes along only on rare occasions, have huge mouths equipped to deal with fish almost as big as themselves.

In the constant 'arms race' between predators and prey it appears that some prey fish, such as crucian carp, may actually develop deeper bodies in waters where there is a greater risk of being eaten by pike. Presumably the idea is to 'put off' any pike that might be considering whether the carp will fit inside its jaws. Indeed, pike prefer to attack *shallow bodied* crucian carp to *deep-bodied* ones, presumably because the latter are more difficult to eat and take longer to hold, turn and swallow. It seems that the development of a deeper body may be the crucian's inbuilt response to the presence of chemicals released into the water by the resident pike (=the smell of pike). Presumably, for these reasons, the use of deeper bodied fish (roach, rudd, bream) as baits may tend to select for bigger pike.

Diet

Although pike prefer to eat other fish, if they can get them, they are pretty adaptable and, as already mentioned, in waters where the pike themselves are the only fish present, they will settle for a meal of insects, snails or leeches, even though they are unable to digest the hard skins and shells of insects and crustaceans. In fact the pike in some 'pike only' Alberta (Canada) lakes fed almost entirely on such creatures. Funnily enough the fish in two of these lakes showed no evidence of cannibalism. Presumably lakes of

this type (like Crag Lough and others along the Whin Sill in Northumberland) could be prime spots for the would-be fly angler in search of his first pike. Of course such situations are fairly unusual and, as a rule, most larger pike are dedicated to eating fish, even if it has to be their own relatives. In fact more than 99 per cent of the stomach contents of River Frome pike consisted of fish.

What sort of fish do pike eat? In the Frome, smaller pike (those less than four years old) fed mostly on dace, gudgeon, minnows, stone loach and migrating salmon smolts (in April–May). Larger pike also ate lots of dace but trout, grayling, eels and smaller pike were quite popular foods. In view of the latter, it is hardly surprising that pike of different sizes rarely live in the same areas.

On the whole big pike like to eat big prey. It takes less energy to catch one good-sized fish than to try and 'fill up' on dozens of minnows or fry. In rivers where salmon and sea trout spawn, the weak, moribund or dead 'kelts' that have spawned are easy prey for big pike. In fact, on the Frome we have caught a number of pike with partly digested salmon kelts wedged in their throats. On one occasion Jerome saw one of his tagged pike grab a salmon kelt and carry it along in its jaws, but in this case the kelt managed to escape. Having said this, the pike must maximize the 'profit' in terms of energy that it obtains from its food. If it expends more effort rushing about after its prey than it gains by eating them then it will not grow and indeed may even lose weight. This is telling us two very important things about fishing for pike.

Firstly, your bait or lure must give the impression of *being easy to catch*. In other words it must move slowly as close as possible to the place where the pike is lying. You can only consistently achieve this by using baits that may be retrieved at a slow pace without plunging to the bottom. Live baits, tethered in front of the pike's lair are obviously good candidates. Unweighted dead baits are also very easy to twitch and flutter right on the predator's nose. Buoyant or slow sinking spoons, plastics, plugs and stick baits (preferably with the trebles modified to singles) are the artificials that most readily fit the bill. On the other hand, heavily weighted or deep diving

Fishing the millstream – often a good bet for small fish if you need a few baits.

Dace are good baits in rivers, but are sometimes inclined to swim at the surface unless weighted down.

Salmon parr, although they are eaten by pike, should never be used as bait.

Rudd are usually easy to catch in lakes and ponds.

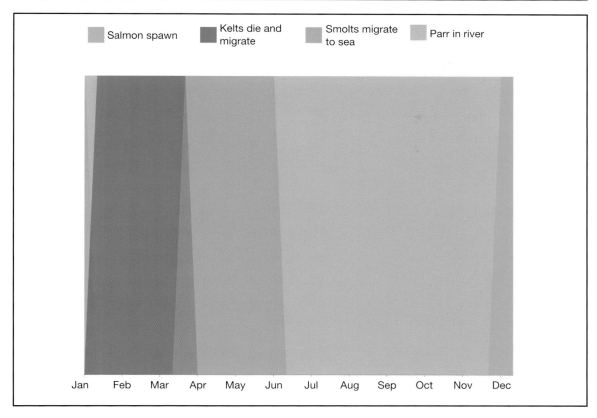

Legend: Salmon spawn | Kelts die and migrate | Smolts migrate to sea | Parr in river

Jan | Feb | Mar | Apr | May | Jun | Jul | Aug | Sep | Oct | Nov | Dec

Vulnerability of salmon to pike attack over the year. The biggest pike are likely to feed on dead and dying kelts early in the New Year; post-spawning trout will be eaten a bit earlier in the season.

lures can be very difficult to keep in the pike's attack zone for long enough to induce a strike. It is probably worth mentioning at this point that the use of live fish as bait is not permitted in all waters and anglers should always check with their local byelaws. Also, mainly because of the risks of spreading disease, it is *never* acceptable or indeed legal to take live or dead baitfish from one water to another.

Secondly, your inducement must appear (to the pike) to be big enough to provide a worthwhile meal. As noted, pike prefer to eat fish that are about one quarter to one third of their own length. Of course, we've all heard of huge pike caught on tiny baits but, in truth, if you want to tempt a fat old pike to exert itself then it is best to use a suitably large-sized bait or lure.

There are times in the lives of fish when they *must* take risks. This is most obvious in species that naturally undergo profound shifts in their way of life, such as eels or salmon; both are particularly prone to these problems. Baby salmon, after spending a year or more in the river and learning how to live the life of a freshwater fish must prepare to go to sea. The transition from river to sea life is pretty grim, Not only do the kidneys have to stop baling out the fresh water that is trying to flood the tissues but the little fish have to learn to drink in order to make good the water that will be sucked out of their bodies by the concentrated brine in which they will be living. Perhaps even more of a problem are the changes in behaviour needed to enable the little silver fish to forget about the heron wading in the shallows, the otter plunging from the bank or the pike lunging from the weed bed and to become aware of the risks of being eaten by coalfish, pollack, cod, bass, terns, gannets, seals, whales and dolphins – what a life (or, more likely, what a death)!

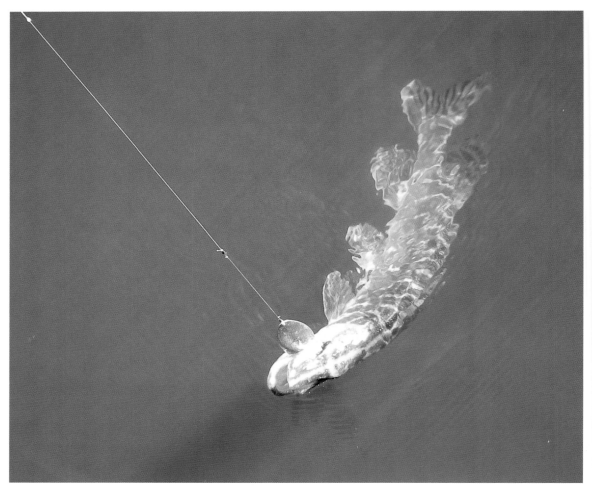

A modest pike caught on a good-sized spoon. These artificials may seem (to the pike) to be bigger than they are and can be fished very slowly.

The trickiest time of all is while the young fish are in the process of switching and moving downstream to the sea as smolts. At this time pike can be a particular hazard. The little fish are having to leave their familiar shallow gravelly home and travel through reach after reach of pike-haunted, weedy pools. Again Finnish scientists tried to get to grips with the situation. They used stocked smolts for their tests (the little silver fish had never seen a pike in their lives so they were at an even greater disadvantage than wild smolts and had to rely on pure instinct to save them). The researchers had already estimated how many pike were in the system and how big they were and, by counting the numbers of smolts in pike stomachs, they were able to get some idea of how many smolts were eaten altogether.

It was estimated that 1,500 pike managed to eat about 13,000 smolts in a single week (getting on for ten per pike). This did not include the effect of smaller pike (less than 40cm in length) which, it was said, may not have been able to catch the smolts (we're sure they could have) or, more likely, may have avoided the smolty places to reduce the risk of being eaten by their larger cousins. It was said that almost the entire diet of the larger pike at this time consisted of salmon smolts. In a stretch where no smolts had been stocked and only wild ones were

This fine perch took a spoon intended for pike while Mike was fishing on the River Stour.

present, the pike were less dependent on them and ate other species of fish. In the Frome it's the small pike that eat most of the smolts.

Of course pike are not the only fish predators in fresh water; perch and zander are also voracious consumers of other fish. As rule competition between species like these may be reduced by differences in their behaviour. Zander tend, for example, to feed in low light conditions when pike are less active. Large, fish-eating perch often favour open water, particularly where there are underwater obstructions to lurk in, while pike have a tendency to hang around weeds and so on. For the pike angler, particularly using lures, there will be a variety of catches. Chub, perch, zander, trout, salmon and even a number of species not normally regarded as predators are all likely to sustain the sport at times.

FEEDING HABITS AND WHAT THEY TELL US

- Pike feed most effectively in clear water with decent light penetration where they can use their excellent eyesight to locate prey fish.
- Strikes on stationary prey often take place shortly after the fish has stopped swimming. They also like their prey to be close before they make a move. So your bait or lure must give the impression of being easy to catch, and must move slowly as close as possible to the place where the pike is lying.
- Big pike like to eat big prey, so your inducement must appear (to the pike) to be big enough to provide a worthwhile meal. The use of deeper bodied fish (roach, rudd, bream) as bait may tend to select for bigger pike.

Perch are partial to small plugs – the pike also like them but they are not ideal pike lures.

A stonking chub caught on a plug by Richard Gardiner.

Trout will also take pike lures.

Salmon, in their winter close season, are particularly susceptible to big pike lures and if caught accidentally should be released at once by unhooking at the water's edge.

7 GRUB UP!

A successful hunter must know the whereabouts and vulnerability of its prey. The activities of pike (and of course those of the good pike angler) must be largely governed by the seasonal changes in prey abundance and availability.

What most pike anglers would like to know, we are sure, is whether there are any short cuts to big catches of large fish. Is there a quick way of deciding where to find them (apart, that is, from trying to sift fact from fiction in the angling literature)? Of course, as with any predator, the key to the whereabouts of pike is the presence of prey fish. Let's look at the seasonal behaviour of some of the main prey species and see if they provide us with any useful clues. Of course you need to know what species are present in the waters you fish and, ideally, which ones are likely to be the main prey of the resident pike.

It might sound obvious, but the first thing to remember is that *fish are fish* wherever they live. In general, the dace of the Dorset Frome will behave more or less like dace in the Tyne, the Trent, the Severn, or indeed any other river. The same thing applies equally to other species. Of course, fish in ponds and lakes are likely to behave somewhat differently to those in rivers and activities in cold northern waters may lag a bit behind those in the sunny south, but the same principles apply.

How can you find out what a particular species does? Well, for a start, you can read what others say in books and magazines. If you do this it will be necessary to distinguish truth from ignorance and fact from fiction – as noted already, not always an easy matter. Secondly, you can try to pick the brains of older, more experienced, anglers. Again you need to select the fishermen who really know their stuff – such

people are few and far between and may be a bit cagey or even downright secretive. There is, however, a third approach.

As we have said, every species of fish has its own favourite habitats and seasonal patterns of behaviour (that's one of the things that makes them different species). What you need to do is learn something about the preferences of each of the pike's 'target' items of diet. This means not only where it lives, when it feeds, what it likes to eat but particularly when it may be most vulnerable to predation. Examples of such times include when prey fish are likely to gather in large numbers, when they are likely to be less alert than usual (e.g. at spawning time, when they are migrating, when they're holed up for the winter or when they're in a feeding frenzy!) and when they may be weaker or more inactive than usual (e.g. after spawning). Simple, eh?

Dace

Take just one example – the dace. River pike love to eat dace. Dace are drift feeders, taking mostly insects such as the larvae of blackflies and caddis flies but they are also partial to bits of plant material. They gather together, frequently in large shoals, in shallow, swift flowing water – not very pikey places you might think. Fortunately, on the River Frome, Dr Stuart Clough spent several years working with Mike and observing the habits of dace by means of radio tracking with tiny tags. Much of what he found out was new and astonishing and forms the basis of the following account. The information is just as valuable to the pike man as to the dace angler.

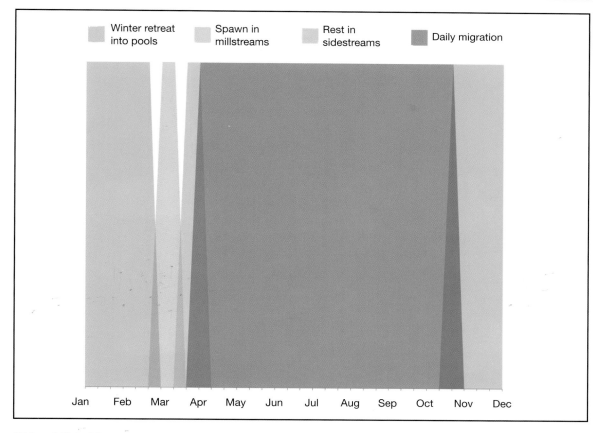

Vulnerability of dace to pike attack over the year. Find the concentrations of dace (or any other prey fish) and the pike will not be far away.

In the hours of daylight, dace will often be loosely shoaled in open areas of clean sandy or gravelly bottom where, presumably, they can generally see the pike coming and avoid becoming a meal for them. At dusk, when drifting insects, which they eat, reach their peak abundance (hence the 'evening rise' of trout fishing lore) the dace will shift, swimming against the current to pools lying downstream of weedy shallows, where the drifting food is thickest. If a pike wants to catch a big dace it will be waiting in or close to such places for them to arrive. To conserve energy, the pike will be out of the main flow in a bankside slack. If possible it will lie beneath overhead cover and/or at the edge of water plants where it can see without being seen. As the light fails the pike will be on the alert. Of course, at dawn, the dace must return to their daytime haunts and again the pike will

be waiting to catch them 'in transit'. Since it will probably have been fasting through the hours of darkness the pike is most likely to be hungry at dawn (sorry, but it means that to give yourself the best chance you may have to be fishing as it gets light).

The biggest shoals of dace form in winter, when the fish drop downstream into relatively deep slow-flowing water. In small rivers this may be near the estuary or river mouth but in larger ones it could simply be the next big pool downstream. Once again the pike will follow (or anticipate) the shoals moving into this deeper water.

At spawning time the dace congregate in shallow, gravel-bedded, side channels (such as mill streams) and of course the pike will have learned this too. Spawning dace, in March, are pretty well preoccupied with the business in

Male (top) and female dace at spawning time (early March). The males feel rougher-skinned and are slimmer than the females. Both seem to be equally popular meals for pike.

hand and much less likely to see the lurking predator, presenting it with the chance of an easy meal. In April, after spawning, many of the weakened dace move into small side stream tributaries to recover from their exertions. Once again the pike will surely not be slow to take advantage of this opportunity and may hang around near such spots.

So there we have it, in rivers with large stocks of dace there is a whole series of events, each allowing the pike (and the pike angler) to capitalize on the chance of a catch. Simple, isn't it? Of course 'close seasons' for fishing may influence your opportunities to fish for pike at some of the prime times and places.

In lakes too there are often daily and seasonal migrations of 'pike food'. Such migrations are a response to the fact that the little animals of the plankton often swim up towards the surface in the hours of darkness. Of course the fish, such as young perch, bream and roach, follow the plankton on which they feed into the upper layers of open water at night. For sure, the resident pike in lakes, although they themselves feed almost entirely along the shore zone of the lake, will be well aware of these migrations and will lie in wait, on the outer margins of weed and reed beds, for the outgoing and returning fish again at dusk and dawn.

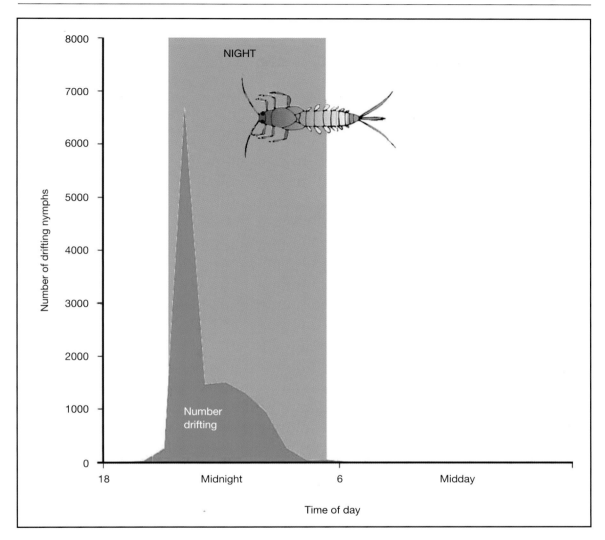

Why are river pike active at dusk? Lots of insects drift in the late evening and prey fish feed on them then (the 'evening rise'), becoming open to pike attack as they do so.

Salmon and Trout

How about another example. Rivers, particularly those in the north and west of Britain, containing salmon and sea trout also provide a number of 'windows of opportunity' for the resident pike. In April and May the little blotchy parr (yearling or older salmonids) turn into silver skinned smolts and migrate downstream towards the sea. This annual migration happens every year. In essence the early (March) running fish move at night in ones, twos and threes,

which probably gives them a measure of protection from marauding pike. However, in April and May, as the days warm up and the water temperature gets above about 12°C, the little silver fish begin to gather into large, tight schools and migrate *in the daytime*. It may be that, at this time of year, the risk of predation in the hours of darkness by returning, nocturnal sea trout (sea trout anglers, please note) is increasing, so the little fish are safer if they move in daylight. Under these conditions the shoals are the smolt's best means of defence against daytime

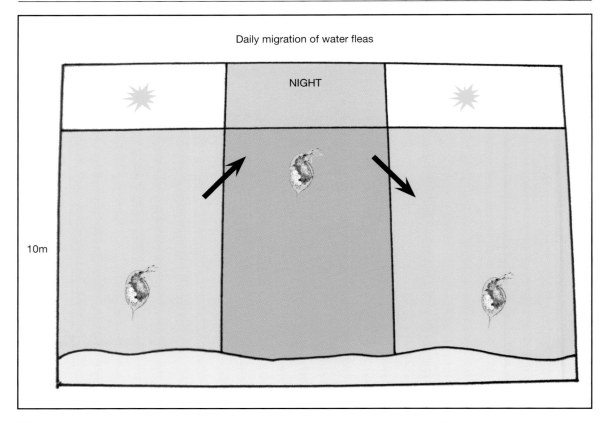

Why are lake pike active at dusk? Plankton rise towards the surface at night and prey fish leave their cover to feed on them – the pike will be waiting.

feeding pike. This defence is not totally effective and in a study on the River Frome, for example, 60 per cent of the pike's food in the month of April consisted of smolts. In contrast, one of the main foods of larger pike in September was adult sea trout as the smaller fish were returning to the river from their feeding grounds in salt water.

Now, a salmon (or trout) smolt weighing, say, 20g and measuring 10cm or so in length is a fairly small (if nutritious) mouthful for a pike and so the main predation on these fish is generally by smaller pike – often less than a year old. The smolts tend to swim downstream following the main flow, so the pike will be waiting for them around projections of the bank or behind rocks or beds of weed where they have shelter from the flow but with easy access to the passing shoals.

Where there is a lake or lakes along the course of a river, smolts, migrating down to the sea,

have to run the gauntlet and may be subject to heavy predation by pike. In one Danish reservoir pike were found to be responsible for 56 per cent of the deaths of tagged, hatchery-reared (i.e. naive) salmon smolts. There is one further twist in this story because if, as is often the case, the smolt migration happens to coincide with pike spawning time, more smolts escape while their persecutors are otherwise occupied with sex.

The incoming trout and salmon, returning from their feeding grounds in the sea, are usually much too big to be eaten by any but the very largest pike. In addition trout are extremely lively fish and so are fairly (but not totally) safe (although in September the returning smaller sea trout may be eaten in considerable numbers). However, after they have completed spawning (November to February, depending on the river) it's a completely different story. Salmon, in particular, are greatly weakened and a lots of them die. Now a five-pound, dead or dying salmon kelt lying on the riverbed or mooching around in the slack water is perfect for a big pike. In rivers with a run of game fish this is a good place and time to fish your big dead bait or outsize, slowly wobbling plug or spoon (if you are allowed to) in search of a real monster. In this case, far from being the villains of the piece (as many game anglers might think), the pike are acting as scavengers, recycling refuse from the riverbed. Of course, a pike that already has a gut full of decomposing salmon may not always be easy to tempt, so you will probably have to be patient.

Other Types of Prey

Where they occur, river lampreys are eaten by pike (although they are protected and should not be caught as baits). Jerome has quite often seen lampreys bearing the scars of a pike attack. Young river lampreys migrate from the river to the sea where they are parasites on other fish. They later return to the river to spawn and at that time they may be devoured by the resident pike – a case of the biter bit!

Pike in lakes are just as opportunistic as their cousins in running water. Perch, which despite their spiny dorsal fins are popular items in the pike's diet, undergo seasonal migrations from inshore areas into deep water. Young perch may be eaten in huge quantities in August, when they are particularly abundant in the marginal shallows. In Windermere, perch are eaten all the year round but again mostly in the spring and summer months (May to September) when they are in shallow water. Charr – relatives of trout and salmon – which are also numerous in the Lake, are found to be of particular importance as food for the local pike in November and December. This is the season when some of the charr swim into the shallows to spawn and no doubt preoccupied, exhausted or moribund charr become easy meat for the pike. Again in Windermere trout are eaten mostly between October and February – when they are spawning or recovering from spawning.

By now you will be getting the message, but just in case you still harbour any doubts about targeting the times and places where bait fish are vulnerable to pike attack, one or two examples of a different kind may help to reinforce the point about the predator 'making hay while the sun shines'. In Lake Thomson, a shallow prairie lake in South Dakota, USA, the pike eat large numbers of leopard frogs in October – just when the frogs are migrating into deeper water to hibernate. Smelt, little silver fish that, like salmon and trout, migrate from the sea into rivers to spawn are eaten in quantity during their post-spawning downstream migration. In a number of other waters smelt and leopard frogs have both been mentioned as seasonally-important pike foods.

Seasonal and Daily Patterns

So, pike do feed with seasonal patterns! In the Arakum reservoirs of Central Asia (where no doubt the spring comes later than ours), they have distinct feeding peaks in April and again in August. The spring peak is associated with spawning aggregations of coarse fish, notably roach. The pike were seen to eat about three or four times their own body weight of food every year, mostly at these 'prime times'. The later summer peak may, in this case, be related to the fact that the fish are trying to pile on weight because they hardly feed at all in the cold winter months. In a Canadian lake, where the stomach contents of almost 30,000 pike were examined, the fish concentrated their feeding on 'trout-perch' in May and June, spottail shiner (a bit like dace or roach) in July, perch in August and September and after that on sticklebacks. So, although there are distinct patterns in when and what pike eat through the year (and no doubt the same sort of thing occurs in the British Isles) these will differ considerably in different parts of the pike's world distribution.

In Polish lakes, shoals of young roach and perch were observed by echolocation. It was found that they swam to the surface of open water to feed on plankton at dusk and returned to the safety of the shallows at dawn. Of course, avoiding predators may not be the only reason for these migrations and spending the day in

Reeds like the ones lining this ditch are prime hiding places for pike.

shallower, warmer water may speed up digestion and growth. However, there is no doubt the pike will be well aware of these movements. Perhaps not surprisingly, in view of these observations, in one European study pike were found to be closer to the shore in daytime than at night.

So, let's consider – why do pike tend to move out into open water at night? It seems that, at least in summer, some prey fish, which spend the daylight hours hiding among inshore vegetation, swim out from the margins as darkness falls. As mentioned above, roach, for example, are known to leave their shoreline haunts in the evening returning again as soon as the sun comes up. Perhaps the pike are just following (or trying to cut off) their potential prey.

Particular individual pike may well become specialist feeders (a bit like 'specimen hunting' anglers). For example, after spawning, while most pike in a dammed river returned to their usual feeding haunts a few appeared to move to areas where they could prey chiefly on sea trout smolts. It has also been demonstrated, as already mentioned, that some pike specialized in catching insects while most were feeding on fish. This may seem a foolish thing to do but presumably these insect feeders will have an advantage at times when fish are hard to come by.

It is impossible to give every example of fish eaten by pike but most coarse fish species spawn in the spring and early summer so you can work out for your own favourite water what is likely to be on the pike's menu at a given time of year and where you could profitably concentrate your effort. Neil Trudgill of the Environment Agency has kindly allowed us to use the following table that he prepared (we have slightly modified it to include pike and salmon).

- The key to the whereabouts of pike is the presence of its prey, so it is important to learn something about the prey's lifestyle – where it lives, when it feeds, what it likes to eat and particularly when it may be most vulnerable to predation.
- Most coarse fish species spawn in the spring and early summer, so you can work out what is likely to be on the pike's menu at a given time of year for your own favourite water and where you could profitably concentrate your effort.

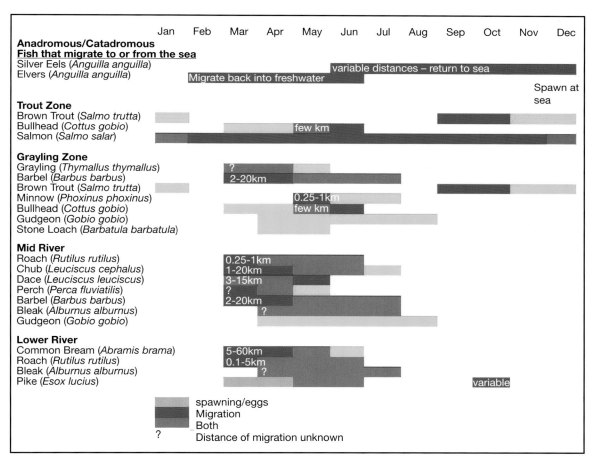

The main spawning seasons of our freshwater species (modified after a diagram by Neil Trudgill). Pike may eat them when they are preoccupied or weakened by these activities.

8 MOVEMENTS AND MIGRATIONS

Do pike stay in the same place for a long? Do they move about a lot? Do they fast? Will they always take an easy meal? These questions are critical to angling success. We have some of the answers.

You have already heard the story of Isaac. How he moved from winter to summer quarters each year. We suppose the question is – do all pike do something similar to this? The answer, of course, is no!

Tagging and Tracking . . .

It's not as easy as it might appear to track fish and many hours (days and weeks) can be wasted in fruitless searches for failed tags. Our own experiences will show you what we mean.

Once we had radio-tagged and released a fish, we needed to use a radio receiver and antenna to find it again. The receiver was a small box hung over a shoulder using a carrying strap. The antenna looked like a little television aerial. The prongs on the antenna were made of thin flexible metal so, if they became bent as you fought your way through bushes and trees, they would snap back into place. This saved hours of 'make do and mend' when we had to work in dense riverbank thickets.

Most of our radio tracking was carried out on the River Frome in Dorset. The Frome is a fairly natural chalk stream fed by rich sources of groundwater. The river channel meanders through lush fields and scrubby woodlands of alder and willow and is free to burst its banks under high flows. At such times the water covers much of the surrounding meadows. The main study area, where the pike were followed, consists of over 2,000m of river (average width about 14m), flowing from west to east. A few miles further on the Frome joins its sister river, the Piddle, before entering the sea at Poole Harbour.

The grassland surrounding the river is part of a former 'flood meadow' system and as a result there are a number of artificial drainage ditches connected to the main river. A millstream, which no longer has a mill, leaves the main river and rejoins within the tracking stretch. An Environment Agency gauging weir, supporting a salmon counter, takes most of the flow of the river and downstream of it is a sizeable weir-pool. The weir itself forms a bit of a potential barrier to fish movement (although pike, dace and mullet often swim up it with ease) but there are no other obstructions downstream of the main study reach.

There are lots of submerged plants in the river consisting mainly of chalkstream water buttercup and various pondweeds. Reeds and grasses form sparse thickets along the muddy banks. Farmland alongside the river is mostly pasture, grazed by cattle and sheep with, here and there, small areas of boggy fen and there are few overhanging willow trees and bushes to provide shade.

In addition to pike, there are a number of other fish in the river, any and all of which are eaten by pike at times, including salmon, brown and sea trout, grayling, minnow, dace, roach, stone loach, eel, bullhead, flounder, sticklebacks, thinlipped mullet and lampreys.

To help us to understand the behaviour of our tagged pike, information about conditions in the river was measured at the gauging weir. Flow was recorded every fifteen minutes,

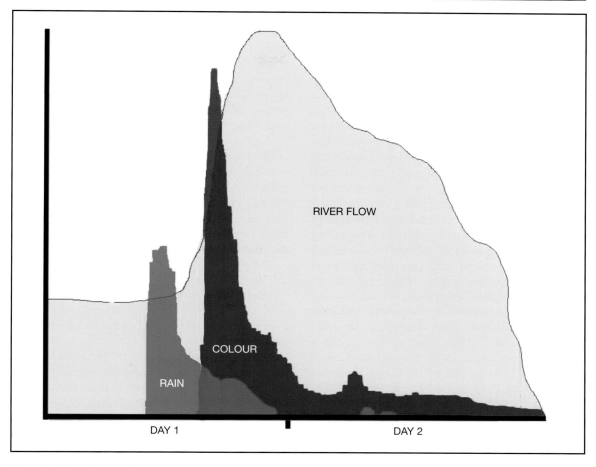

How the River Frome colours up after rain. The water begins to clear and the pike may come on the feed, well before the peak of flow. Many other rivers may show similar patterns but the timing will vary.

these data being supplied by the Environment Agency. Water temperature was also recorded every fifteen minutes. Daily mean discharges (water flows) and temperatures were calculated from the quarter-hourly records.

Most of the time we were lucky enough to be tracking in the middle of the countryside, so our unusual appearance – dressed in chest waders and waving television aerials about – didn't attract a lot of attention other than from fields of cows or sheep. On the rare occasions when we did meet people, they would often ask whether we could pick up the BBC or ITV on our equipment. In fact there are strict rules about radio tracking. All wildlife tags used in the UK broadcast over a fixed set of frequencies to make sure they don't interfere with other radio users. This

means that our equipment couldn't accidentally mess up the police, ambulance or fire service emergency calls. It does also mean that you can't stroll along listening to Wogan (Who on earth would want to? – Sorry, Jerome says, 'I like Wogan!') while you try to find your fish.

Although we didn't meet many people when out tracking, the county's Police Headquarters was located only a mile or two from our stretch of river. This meant that, despite the idyllic rural location, on a couple of occasions a police helicopter circled overhead to see what we were up to! The local livestock also made tracking a bit more interesting at times. We would often have to pass through a herd of bullocks, owned by the local tenant farmer. The bullocks, being very curious animals, would often come up close to see what was happenning. It wasn't unusual to be standing on the riverbank, absorbed in what we were doing, only to look up and find a bullock licking the end of the antenna. This was another time when the flexibility of the prongs of our aerials came in useful as they were able to withstand lots of bovine attention without breaking. Cattle are surprisingly light on their feet and their approach is often unnoticed so it can be a bit disturbing to be nudged in the back by a wet, slimy muzzle when you are absorbed in fiddling with the dials on the receiver and leaning out over six feet of water.

Before we started tracking real fish we had to get some practice and gain confidence regarding the exact whereabouts of fish that we couldn't see. The idea was to find tags that had been hidden for us by our 'pals'. These were often placed in a weighted carp sack, which was tied to a convenient branch or tree stump and then thrown into the river (tags are expensive so the knots had to be secure). The range of a tag is less when it is underwater than on land, so it was vital for us to be able to locate tags that were actually in the river. It's a fairly nerve-wracking experience setting out from the laboratory for the first time to recover a tag, when you know that the whole of the three-year study depends on whether you can find the thing again. It doesn't help when you think that the guy who hid the tag is watching you out of the window and pissing himself with laughter as you head off in the wrong direction.

Most of the radio tags we used had signals that could be picked up from about 100m away. As we've mentioned, each tag transmitted on a unique frequency, so we could always tell the pike apart, even if we had lots of tagged fish in the river at the same time.

The majority of our tracking was done on foot. We would walk along the riverbank (through ditches, swamps and brambles) and then, when we picked up a signal (a little repeated bleep rather like the microwave telling you that your coffee's ready), would turn around in a circle to work out where the strongest signal (loudest bleep or better still biggest deflection of a needle on the dial of the receiver) was coming from. By walking in the direction of the strongest response, we were able to get pretty close to

most fish. The closer we got to a tag, the clearer the signal became until, when we were very near, the signal seemed to be all around and it was difficult to determine its exact position. At this stage, to pinpoint the fish, we resorted to tactics like detuning away from the tag's frequency, adjusting the gain on the receiver, or turning the antenna onto its side to reduce the signal strength. These little tricks meant we could work out directions again and home in precisely on the fish's position. Once we were really close, it was usually possible to work out the pike's exact location by 'triangulation'; walking 5–10m upstream and downstream of where we thought the fish was and seeing where the directions of strongest signal crossed.

. . . and What It Can Tell Us

Pike are pretty sedentary animals and for hours at a stretch don't move about much (they are 'lurking predators', after all) so that when we went out tracking, we would often find our fish pretty much in the area where we had last left them. Sometimes though, the fish weren't where we expected and it was necessary to really search for them. The problem now was that to find our pike again we needed to get within a 100m or so of it. Although we knew the fish had swum off somewhere (unless, as happened on the odd occasion, it had been caught and removed from the river by some game angler, otter, mink or other predator), we hadn't got a clue whether it had gone upstream or downstream. The only thing to do was pick a direction and start walking. Sometimes we'd walk for many miles before hearing that welcome little beep that meant we had found it again.

On odd occasions, to save our feet and waders, we would use a small inflatable boat to cover long sections of river quickly in the search for a 'missing' fish. One person would row whilst the other scanned about with the antenna – not always the easiest thing to do in a confined space. Pokes in the eye were frequent and after sundry whacks on the head it was obvious that we had yet another reason to be grateful for the flexibility of the antenna prongs.

We were also forced to resort to tracking by

boat during the foot and mouth outbreak in 2001. Obviously no one was allowed to tramp through fields of livestock at this time, due to the restrictions on walking over agricultural land. The local farmers, bless them, let us float past in our boat as long as we took great care to launch and recover the dinghy well away from their pastures.

In any event, tracking from a boat was not ideal, because it was never easy to tell where the pike were with as much accuracy as when we tracked from terra firma (or terra squelchy at any rate). The best we could manage was to record the rough location of a pike as we went floating past (sometimes at speed) as the current was often too strong for us to hold the boat in one place for any length of time. We couldn't use an engine, because some of the riffles we were travelling over were too shallow for a prop and in any case there was a strong chance of 'putting the wind up' the poor old pike.

The local swans (which are numerous) didn't always know what to make of our voyages as they were not used to seeing boats on *their* river. Often the swans (usually in pairs) would swim ahead of us, going faster and faster until finally taking fright and flying off. On one occasion, on the lower river near Wareham, we must have been driving a herd of about thirty swans ahead of us, all of them switching between paddling downstream and looking nervously over their shoulders. The herd rounded a sharp bend only to meet a pleasure boat full of holidaymakers coming the other way. Sandwiched between the two boats, the swans panicked and decided to make a break for it. After thrashing the river to foam with a huge amount of noisy flapping they took off and disappeared into the distance (it's not easy for a bird as big as a swan to 'unstick' itself from the water). In the breeding season swans become quite aggressive and then it's not so much a case of herding them as battening down the hatches, ducking (or should it be swanning) down and fending off their attacks with an oar.

We carried on tracking throughout prolonged flooding in the winter of 2000. At this time the fields around the Frome were under water for several weeks at a time, but we took precautions to make things as safe as possible. Health and

safety regulations already dictated that everyone wore lifejackets the whole time we were out and it was essential to make sure that someone always knew where we were going. For obvious reasons there was no tracking at night during this period.

In fact it was really hard work tracking during the floods. A flooded river looks very much like a big lake, but it's not until you start paddling about in the flooded fields that you realize that it is all flowing. Walking (=wading) a couple of miles in a thigh-deep torrent to 'round up' and locate all our fish wasn't easy and there was always the additional risk of stepping into a ditch or even over the riverbank. It was well worth the effort though, because some of the most interesting results came during this time, showing how important flood plains can be for fish in general and pike in particular.

The radio tags were really pretty good at telling us where our pike were and what they were doing, but they still had limitations. We could get a very good idea of where fish were, across the width of the river, but it wasn't always possible to tell just how deep down they were. Were they sitting underneath streaming *Ranunculus* weed, looking out over gravel shoals for unsuspecting prey fish to pass them by? Were they using the contours of the river bed to find shelter from the flow? Were they hovering just beneath the water surface or lurking in mid water amid the submerged roots of a tree? It was often hard to tell.

Having decided that we wanted to try to pin down *exactly* where each pike was, an attempt was made to combine radio tracking and snorkelling. It has been reported elsewhere that small pike are quite bold and not easily scared by the presence of humans in diving gear. However, we can state with some confidence that approaching and observing larger fish in this way is not easy! Whilst we read scientific papers in which researchers had swum through lakes recording the positions of every pike they found, we were rarely able to make any decent underwater observations of our tagged river fish.

The idea was that one person would stand on the bank with the radio equipment yelling instructions to the swimmer in the water, who would valiantly dive down time and again to

Trying to locate tagged pike underwater – not an easy matter.

search for the fish. The camouflage of the pike was so good that you had to be virtually on top of the fish to see it (pity the poor old dace or roach!). Although we only tried this in summer low flows, you had to swim pretty hard just to stay in place, which made stealthy approaches to the fish next to impossible. On the few occasions when we did manage to get close, the tracker would usually hear the tag switch to its rapid bleep mode, indicating that *Esox* was well aware of the presence of the clumsy swimmer and was already making him (or her) self scarce. All the swimmer would see was a plume of mud, stirred up by the fish as it 'took to the hills'.

By now you will have gathered that radio tracking is far from being a simple way of finding out about the secret life of the pike. In fact it's a very time-consuming and fiddly business. At times we could walk around the main study stretch and find all of our fish in a couple of hours, but often tracking had to be very intensive. For a two-week period every few months, we would go out and locate each of our fish in the morning, in the middle of the day and again in the evening. We would also, at times, track several fish each hour, for the whole of the day and through the night too. Occasionally, we would stay with one fish continuously for a lengthy period, to see what it was getting up to. None of this would have been even remotely possible without our friends, the dedicated bunch of scientists and students who helped, either by going out and tracking or by rowing us down the river during the times when we had to use the boat.

Tracking Studies

Radio tracking is not the only way to locate fish. It is also possible to use ultrasonic tags, which have been employed successfully in lakes, although they are less useful in rivers where the noise of weirs and rapids can mask their signal. Canadian pike have been tagged by means of these gadgets, which were inserted into the belly after a spot of surgery. The only tagged fish that died after this tagging were ones that were caught (as food) by anglers. These fish were all found to be well healed and had no infections around the tagging scars. They had all grown normally and were, obviously, fit enough to take angler's lures.

Some studies on radio-tagged pike were carried out in a huge river and lake system – the Minto Flats – in Canada. Almost 100 fish were fitted with radio tags and because of the great distances involved they were tracked from a Cessna 185 aircraft flying at low altitude. Despite many tag 'failures' and 'lost' pike, results showed that some fish averaged as much as 3km per day and covered distances of well over 100km in all (another study followed a single tagged pike over a distance of 322km). Of course, not all pike go in for this long-distance swimming (it would be difficult for them in a small pond!), but it would clearly be a serious error to assume that they are *always* in the same places.

Although it does not apply to British waters, it is interesting to note that the 'Minto Flats' pike often swam particularly long distances at the start of the freeze-up in October and that (perhaps not surprisingly) movement declined as winter progressed. There was a second period of high activity during the spring thaw. Other studies have shown the same sort of seasonal pattern. It was concluded that, in winter, the fish generally shifted into areas where oxygen concentrations remained high and this could be a pointer to finding fish in autumn when decaying plants and fallen leaves reduce oxygen levels.

Turbulence caused by weirs, riffles or the wind blowing on the surface may aerate the water and give some clues where to fish in these conditions. In other situations oxygen generated by growing waterweeds during bright sunny days may also have a similar attraction for the pike.

In the Eleven Mile Reservoir of Canada it was found (again by ultrasonic tagging) that most pike movements were around the shore, with very few pike trying to cross the lake. As in other still waters, most pike lived in the weed beds near the edges. Pike showed a strong peak of activity in the spring, presumably round about spawning time, and in the warmer months of the year, like the fish of the Frome, they had peaks of movement at dawn and at dusk. This reservoir was interesting because the pike used to feed mostly on 'suckers' until these fish were largely replaced by stocked rainbow trout. The pike, being typically quick to exploit a new food source, then switched their diet from suckers to mainly trout.

To get extra information radio tags have been used in combination with small heart rate monitors to find out what pike in a loch were doing. Just like us, the hearts of pike beat faster when they become excited. In loch pike, most of the feeding activity (bursts of fast heartbeats) took place in the hours of daylight. The rate of heartbeats stayed higher than normal while the pike were processing their latest meal. As it turned out, usually the pike had digested whatever they managed to catch (in this case young perch) by the following morning. No doubt in (most) waters, where the pike are inclined to eat bigger fish, it could take several days for them to digest and absorb a large meal.

Apart from the tracking studies, the fish populations of the lower River Frome in southern England were extensively studied by Dr Richard Mann and his colleagues, and much was discovered about the diet, numbers and age structure of the pike. However, until recently very little was known about the movements or activity and feeding patterns of these fish. As already mentioned, there have been quite a few studies on pike activity in lakes and ponds but the interactions between pike and their prey in rivers is only poorly understood.

A tagged pike. The tag is inserted through a small incision in the body wall, which is stitched with 'dissolving thread' and treated with disinfectant and antibiotics.

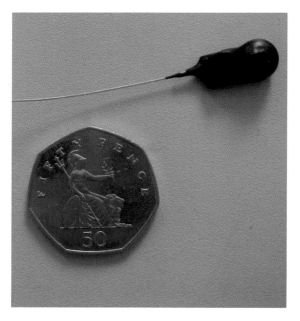

A small external radio tag with a whip aerial. These are attached with a couple of stitches and used to track the movements of dace and other small fish including young pike.

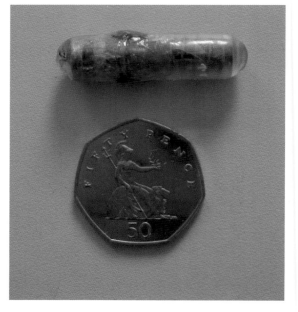

A small internal radio tag used for tracking smaller pike.

A larger internal radio tag used for 'catchable' pike and incorporating an 'activity switch'. The red sticky tape holds a magnet in position to deactivate the tag. The magnet is removed before use.

Over 8,500 tracking observations were made on feeding activity of Frome pike by using the motion-sensing radio tags. Of course, there is a bit of a problem in keeping track of the behaviour of individual fish day after day, so the behaviour of the pike was recorded for periods of several days at a time by means of special automatic monitoring equipment consisting of a recorder and a fixed aerial. These were set up near the known positions of particular pike in the river. Pike activity bursts can be grouped into two types – short darts lasting less than five seconds and those of longer duration. The fish may move in short sharp rushes (less than five seconds) at any time of the day or night but movements of longer duration, between five seconds and one minute in length (it was shown by monitoring artificially fed pike that these are usually feeding events) are very irregular and are often followed by an entire day or more of doing little or nothing. For 95 per cent of the time the pike are more or less inactive. Feeding activity shows distinct patterns over twenty-four hours, and there is a bit of seasonal variation related to sunrise and sunset times.

Dr Stuart Clough's radio tracking of dace (an important pike food), also on the River Frome, using tiny tags, has shown that shoals undertake active migrations in the river at dawn and dusk in the summer months. This may be related to avoidance of pike predation. It has also been shown that predators have an advantage at the change of light when stalking shoaling prey. However, no one knows whether pike activity patterns reflect this potential advantage at low light conditions.

Pike are usually described as 'ambush predators'. However, whether they attack their prey from a single, regular ambush site, or whether they move between several potential 'lairs' had not been well established for river pike. In lakes there is already some evidence that the fish move about between ambush sites. Pike are adapted for rapid acceleration rather than prolonged swimming and it was thought that in rivers, where they often encounter strong flows, they might be less active hunters. By continuously monitoring pike activity in the Frome an attempt was made to answer this and other questions.

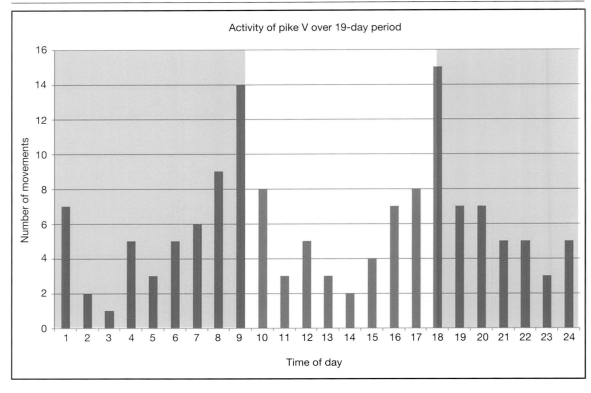

Are pike really *active at dawn and dusk? Just look at the movement peaks of tagged pike V over a period of nineteen days.*

Twenty-four hour tracking made it clear that the pike in the River Frome were generally most active round about dawn and dusk. Data from several fish confirmed these dawn/dusk activity peaks. At spawning time male pike may partly forgo this dawn and dusk pattern to be active throughout the daylight hours. Some pike (but only some) used different regions of the river at different times of year, returning each spring to the same 'spawning area'. In these cases, as already noted, their return to the spawning grounds usually seemed to be triggered by flood conditions. Based on the evidence from the Frome it seems that pike in running water adopt a very mobile hunting strategy and often range about the river from one good 'pitch' to another before carrying out active attacks on prey. Given the energy needed to move against the flow, the use of such a mobile hunting strategy by river pike is a little surprising.

The movement of ten radio-tagged adult pike was investigated in the River Gudenå, a slow flowing Danish stream joining up a number of lakes. (Mike did quite a bit of fishing there some years ago and says that it is not unlike some of the rivers connecting the Norfolk Broads.) The pike typically spent long periods in the submerged weeds, making occasional short (feeding?) excursions to nearby areas. The pike were more active and moved greater distances during a short spell of increasing temperature in early winter. In spring, at spawning time (March to May in this Danish river), they again shifted about, even though the normal places in which they lived were apparently quite suitable for spawning. At this time of year some of the females travelled quite long distances, presumably to spots where they had spawned successfully before.

More tagging studies on pike were carried out in the Kajaaninjoki River (flowing into a very large lake) in Finland to see whether these fish were actually as sluggish as some other work seemed to show. Forty pike were tagged and tracked (quite a task) in the May–June period (the spawning season in this part of Finland) to see whether breeding activity had any influence on their behaviour. In this case less than half of the tracked fish hung about in the places where they had been captured and tagged but two dozen of them swam into the lake after spawning. It is interesting that these pike actually homed and many of the spawning fish returned to the same spawning grounds in the following year. The larger pike were the ones that moved about most and all the tagged fish tended to shift more in the warmer summer months.

The Effects of Being Angled

Of course in the UK, catch-and-release angling of pike is normal. What effect does this have on the fish? The internal tags used for most pike work don't 'unbalance' the fish at all, but it is still worth trying to establish whether the pike are 'perturbed' by being tagged in addition to the possible impact of being removed from the water by electric-fishing or by hook and line. For pike anglers, of course, the crunch is whether catch-and-release fishing adversely affects the fish. Radio tracking of twenty pike was used to test the effect of catch-and-release in a previously unfished lake in north-eastern Germany. Pike, after being caught (again by electric-fishing) and tagged, were given two weeks to recover in the wild (by which time tracking had shown that their behaviour was, as far as could be established, absolutely normal) before being recaptured by angling and again released and tracked.

The only obvious effect of being angled (live baits, dead baits and lures were used) was that the pike did not move about much in the period shortly after they were caught and released but within a day or two at most they seemed to be completely back to normal. It was thought that the initial reduced activity of the fish might have been caused by the stress of being played and removed from the water. It is known that 'angled' fish show the same sort of changes in body chemistry (blood glucose, lactic acid, etc.) that occurs in athletes after exertion and it would be surprising if they didn't take a while to

recover from their efforts. It is also possible that the pike are essentially 'laying low' to reduce the risk of predator attack until they have fully recovered their faculties. In essence, providing the fish are handled with reasonable care, the effects of being 'angled' are short-term and reversible.

Overall, pike were tracked for one day a week over seven months. In a nutshell, fish stayed closer to the shore and moved about less in the first week after being caught. After that it was 'business as usual'. It was also confirmed that the pike preferred to live in and around reed beds and avoided open water.

How Far Will Pike Travel?

The fish moved about more in summer, and were again (as in the Frome) most active in twilight periods (dawn and dusk). In winter pike chose habitats closer to shore and showed no peaks of activity. At this time of the year the pike avoided shallow weed free areas. In summer, submerged weed beds were again preferred to open water. Bigger pike tended to be further from the shore and to move about more than small ones.

Further studies on a German lake have shown that pike have their own little preferred hunting areas within such still waters. Each of the twelve female pike tagged normally hung about within a fairly small part of the lake (usually much less than 50×50m square). In winter, after the weeds had died back, the fish tended to wander about a bit more widely in search of prey but still they remained within their 'home ranges'. Eight of the fish were recaptured by angling and moved to the opposite side of the lake – all quickly returned to their previous 'home'. Obviously it was worth the risk of a long swim to be on familiar ground. The longest time it took to find the way back was less than six days and the shortest only four hours. Most fish managed to home in less than three days.

In the Lake District, the pike of Windermere have been studied in great detail. In this large lake every 100m square will hold something like five pike. Of course they are not spread about like currants in a cake and we can now be sure

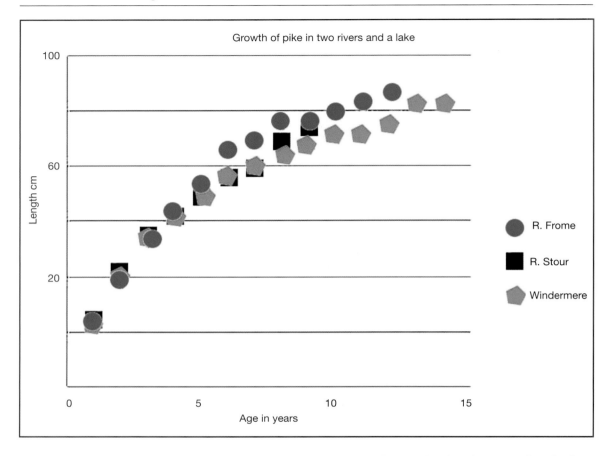

Pike growth in two rivers and a lake. All the fish start off growing at a similar rate, but then the Frome pike take the lead. The Windermere pike survive longer.

that most of these will be concentrated along the shallower, weedy margins with large stretches of open water holding hardly any. For about forty years (up to 1985) the pike of this lake were experimentally fished every winter by gill nets. Over the years the numbers of pike present went up and down and lots of factors were found to be involved. For example, more small pike (less than 20cm long) were devoured by larger pike in cold years when the growth of the young ones was slowed down. In the late 1960s the perch in Windermere were devastated by disease and most of them died. After this the young pike, which had up to that point pretty well depended on small perch as food, struggled to make ends meet and their numbers fell. However, on the whole, the numbers of pike are fairly stable and don't usually fluctuate anything like as much

as do those of prey fish such as perch, roach or dace.

The effects of global warming on pike and other fish have also been studied in Windermere since the early 1980s. It is significant that over fifty years of water temperature records starting in 1957, 2004 to 2006 were the warmest years of all. A sort of 'bottleneck' divides Windermere into two basins and since the 1980s there have been more and fatter pike in the north basin than in the south, possibly because the growing season is longer and the conditions for growth are nearer to ideal there (more oxygen, warmer water and a decline in numbers of charr in the south basin). It is known that charr provide a major boost in the diet of the pike when they move inshore to spawn in late autumn. There has also been an explosion of roach (originally

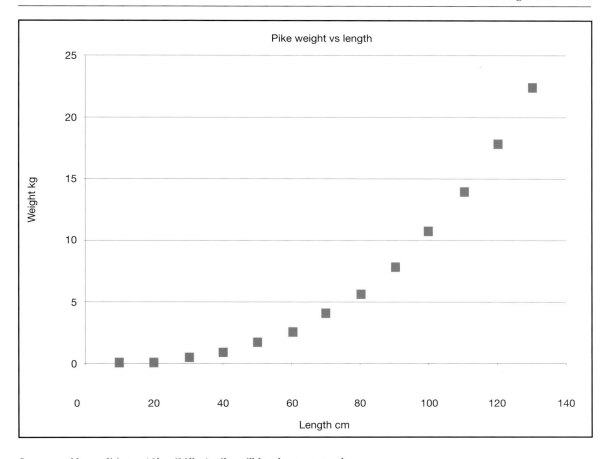

In reasonable condition a 10kg (20lb+) pike will be about a metre long.

introduced long ago as live baits by pike anglers) in both basins, but although these fish are eaten they have not yet become the main foodstuff of the pike in the lake.

- In winter, fish generally move into areas where oxygen concentrations remain high. Pike seem to prefer high concentration of oxygen, so turbulence caused by weirs, riffles or the wind blowing on the surface may aerate the water and give some clues where to fish in these conditions. Oxygen generated by growing waterweed on sunny days may also have a similar attraction for pike.
- Pike do not move about much in the period shortly after being caught and released but studies show that within a day or two they seem to be completely back to normal.

9 TREAT 'EM OR EAT 'EM

In the UK, catch-and-release is the norm for all pike angling. In many other parts of the world they are regarded as pests or even taken home for dinner.

The Pros and Cons of Pike

Despite our love of pike as an angler's fish, there are some places in the world where they are regarded as a menace. We should realize that pike 'control' is an option, depending on the type of fishery you're trying to create. Natural, sustainable fisheries, like some of those that the Environment Agency is restoring (in Yorkshire rivers at least) do not need pike control. Several studies have shown there was a large impact on prey fish populations when pike were introduced outside of their natural range and were therefore acting like an invasive species.

In some fisheries a few introduced pike might help matters, for example in massively over-stocked silver-fish ponds, where the fish all have really poor growth rates and most are of the same (small) size. A few smallish (unisex if possible to prevent breeding) pike could help thin out the numbers of little fish and give the prey a chance to develop to a larger size. Of course it may be difficult to persuade anglers that sacrificing some fish to a predator can improve the fishery. One of the problems is that there are huge differences in scientists' ideas of the amount of fish that pike must devour to keep them going (one such estimate suggests that a young pike in its first year could each eat as many as 500–600 coarse fish fry) but, even taking the lowest values of consumption, the predators can have a fair old impact on prey fish populations.

Just what effect do predators such as pike have on other species? When muskellunge (a type of pike found in North America) were introduced to two lakes containing perch, the number of perch in one lake decreased from more than 30,000 to *too few to count* within a year. In the other lake it took three years for the same sort of decrease to occur. On a slightly different tack, zander were introduced to a lake already containing both pike and perch. The three species 'rubbed along together' nicely with the introduction having little impact on the resident pike. Small perch, however, became the main prey for all three species and they were driven from the open water to live in the shallower margins. Ultimately, the overall result was fewer large perch.

When pike (our species of pike) were introduced into a Nebraska (Canada) lake, within four years perch, bluegill and bass numbers had decreased dramatically and although the remaining bass were bigger than before, both the perch and bluegills were smaller.

Obviously if pike can eat so many wild fish it is likely that they can make serious inroads into the numbers of artificially stocked trout (the flash and vibrations must be like a dinner gong when they are released). Reservoirs like Chew Valley have shown how pike thrive and grow fat in such circumstances. For centuries attempts have been made to reduce the numbers of pike in trout waters.

Pike Management

In chalk streams, which these days are usually more or less artificially sustained by stocking with trout, there is (and there certainly was in times past) an almost fanatical, evangelical approach to pike removal. Pike were (and often still are) regarded as 'vermin' in these rivers. Electric-fishing, trapping, harpooning, netting, noose-wiring and even shooting with shotguns have all been used in years gone by to try to diminish the numbers of pike. On a stretch of the Wiltshire River Avon a concerted effort was made to remove pike by electric-fishing every year. From the 1960s to the 1980s the average size of the pike removed using all legal methods was about five-and-a-half pounds. Subsequently, by assiduous electric-fishing, this weight was halved. One clear effect of removing these pike was to greatly enhance the numbers of dace and grayling (which were also removed by electric-fishing but much less effectively than was the case with pike).

In the 1980s a colleague of ours, Dr Richard Mann, investigated the pike 'management strategy' for this Avon fishery to see whether it was in fact worth all the effort. Richard and his team tagged many of the pike in the stretch so that they could be recognized if they were later recaptured during the annual cull. As a result of the tagging it was estimated that about 50 per cent of the sizeable pike were removed each year. However, it was not simply a case of fishing them out. Pike swam back in from outside the stretch, more of those remaining survived (because of reduced cannibalism by the bigger pike) and the numbers removed by anglers decreased, all of which made up, to some extent, for those taken out by the cull. The average weight of baby pike (less than a year old) in the reach more than doubled during the five-year study, probably because the fish had been thinned out, but the older pike continued to grow at much the same rate as they had before. It was decided that it was probably almost impossible to remove pike totally from such a river, but the numbers could be reduced by a fair amount. Removal of large pike improved the trout fishing as long as *only* good-sized trout (too big to be eaten by small pike) were stocked. Understandably, after pike removal less trout stocking was needed to keep up the quality of the fishing.

What effect would it have on the other fish present if all (or most of) the pike *were* removed from a water? You'd think, from what we've just said, that it could be pretty dramatic – and you'd

be right. Occasionally the chance to investigate such a change crops up. In Lake Arungen, there was a huge increase in the numbers of larger pike that were being caught and removed by netting. The impact of this pike removal on the numerous roach and perch present was observed. Perhaps not surprisingly (in view of their cannibal tendencies) extraction of the large pike first resulted in a mini-explosion of small ones. At the same time the numbers of young (small) roach and perch (now being eaten by the small pike) diminished significantly. The roach and perch both tended to occupy the same areas of the lake but this was more obvious before the large pike had been removed. The prey fish also changed what they were eating after pike were removed, with roach specializing in eating detritus (dead material) and plankton, while the perch went more for fish and plankton animals. The focused feeding by prey fish on animal plankton after pike removal was, at least partly, due to the massive increase in this plankton during this time, which resulted from the reduced numbers of small roach and perch, these having been thinned out by the burgeoning numbers of small pike (and of larger, fish-eating perch). Clearly the culling or exploitation of large pike can result in big knock-on changes in lake fisheries, but not always in the way you might expect.

Of course, the preferred size of fish eaten by a pike will depend to some extent on how big the pike is or, more correctly, on how big the pike's mouth (what scientists call its 'gape') is. The pike in the lakes containing fewer roach and perch had less fish to feed on so they did not grow as big but they did have larger mouths for their size than in the lakes where prey were more numerous but smaller.

As a contrast to the policy of pike removal, in the west of the USA these fish have sometimes been introduced to fisheries, often with disastrous effects, and strenuous efforts are then made to wipe them out. On the other hand, the effects of pollution, global warming, dam building, water level changes and general loss of suitable habitat have often drastically reduced the numbers of pike in otherwise suitable lakes and rivers. In some cases pike anglers have done the damage themselves; they tend to catch the largest fish in a lake or river and if these are intentionally (people eat them) or accidentally killed or removed (effectively they are 'overfished'), it may result in the remaining fish being, on average, much smaller.

The Effects of Angling

Even the normal catch-and-release angling that we do in the UK may affect the movements and feeding patterns of pike. So, what does a pike actually do after you've carefully unhooked it and lovingly returned it to the water? As already mentioned, radio tagging suggests that your fish may tend to 'mope' for a little while after you release it and is less likely to move away from the shore than it was before capture but it will still sit about in reed and weed beds just like any other pike. However, the good news is that the fish rapidly get over their experience and within a couple of days they will be back to their good old lurking, lunging, predatory habits. Of course, as with all aspects of fishing, nothing is black and white. Every fish behaves differently and most pike anglers have probably (like us) recaptured pike that they had returned only minutes or hours earlier.

Scientists have looked into the influence of fishing methods (bait and lure size and type, and body size, injury, and handling time) for pike catches and welfare. They have shown that the type and size of bait used for pike makes a real difference to the size of the fish caught (generally big baits for big fish). Tactics also affect whereabouts in the mouth (or elsewhere) the hooks are likely to lodge. Deep hooking in the gills or throat, which could sometimes injure or kill the pike, was found to be more likely when fishing with natural baits, soft plastic shads, jigs, and spoons than with spinners or plugs. Small baits, less than 7.5cm in length, were more likely to hook the fish in the gills and less likely to hook them in the upper jaw than were larger baits. It was also more of a palaver and took longer to remove hooks from the gill arches than from other parts of the mouth. Deep hooked pike of all sizes were more likely to bleed than those hooked superficially whatever sort of bait or tactics were being used. Not many pike died from the immediate effects of being caught but

those that died later were most likely to be the ones that had bled when they were caught.

Of course, it should already be well known to pike anglers that big baits tend to catch big fish but it's good to have scientific proof that large artificial lures and large natural baits will reduce numbers of small pike hooked. On the other hand it was said that using natural fish baits could result in more fish being deeply hooked, and increase the numbers injured or made to bleed. To us this seems to confirm the value of avoiding the use of small, multi-hooked lures in waters where pike are present (we don't do it any more if we can avoid it – pike will sometimes, of course, take lures intended for perch, chub or trout) and particularly it emphasizes the potential value of debarbed circle hooks as a means of presenting live or dead baits for pike.

In the USA studies were carried out on how easy pike were to catch. Eight ponds in Missouri were stocked with equal numbers of pike (Northern pike), muskies (muskellunge) and tiger muskies (a hybrid beween the other two species). The fish were fed on goldfish and fathead minnows and were then caught by spinning with Mepps spinners. The individual fish had been marked so that they could be identified when they were caught. For a couple of months in mid-summer, when the water was warm, the three types of fish did not bite well. On the whole the Northern pike (the type found in British waters) were much more easily caught than the other two predators and they did not learn to avoid lures, even when they had been hooked repeatedly. On average about one fish was caught for every hour's spinning and even though the same numbers and sizes of each 'species' were present the overall catch consisted of nine muskies, twelve tigers and thirty-eight pike. One of the pike was caught seven times and all of them were caught at least once. Very few of the, admittedly smallish, fish used in this study, died after they had been caught and returned. Only one pike was killed by being caught and others, even those that were gill-hooked or throat-hooked, recovered completely with no further treatment. Some Dutch 'catchability' experiments with somewhat larger pike showed, in contrast, that they were quite difficult to catch more than once on artificial lures but they never learned to avoid live baits.

A pike caught on a Eurovibe lure. Small multi-hook baits like this can cause considerable damage to the fish.

A pike well hooked in the jaw on a 4/0 circle hook. The hook often slides round behind the maxilla after lodging in the 'scissors'.

This pike is jaw-hooked on a circle hook, but the large barb has caused minor damage to the jawbone. We now flatten the barbs of such hooks.

Large, soft plastic lures like this often come armed with a single hook above and a large treble hanging from a ring below. We find that removing the treble makes little difference to the catching efficiency.

Predatory fish in general, because of the ferocious manner in which they attack lures and baits, and the relatively large hooks that are used, may be badly hooked and can die if poorly handled. Largemouth bass, for example, are known to be less likely to survive if roughly treated and this is worse if temperatures are high. As a rule it is found that lure-caught fish are less likely to be killed than those caught on hooks with natural baits. Presumably this is largely due to the fact that the latter are more likely to result in deep hooking and consequent damage to the fish. Most of the work on hooking mortality has been carried out in the USA and not much of it involved pike. However, the results (with a pinch of salt) can probably be applied to our favourite fish.

First – a quick look at the American experience. In an experiment with smallmouth bass, those caught on minnow-baited single hooks suffered 11 per cent mortality while none of those caught on spinners died. Some of these fish were caught more than once. More cutthroat trout caught on worm-baited hooks died than did those caught on spinners. Sadly, this type of information is often used as an excuse for restricting the use of natural baits, whereas with appropriate modification of tactics there should be no difference between fish caught on live or dead baits and those caught on artificial lures or flies. Deep-hooked or otherwise badly hooked or bleeding fish were much more likely to succumb than those hooked in the jaw. Fish hooked in the jaw on worm baits were no more likely to die than those caught using other methods, so it would seem likely that the use of jaw hooking technology, such as circle hooks, can only be beneficial. In fact, in our experience, pike hooked on small lures armed with treble hooks or even on flies with single J-hooks are more likely to be deeply hooked than those caught on appropriate baited single hooks.

Experience and Preference

We've all heard of 'educated' fish and how the carp/roach/bream/or what have you are more difficult to catch in hard-fished waters. Could pike (or other predators) become educated in the same fashion? American researchers found that artificially-bred and reared tiger muskies (as mentioned earlier, they are the offspring of female muskellunge and male pike – we'll just call them 'pike'), fed on pellets, don't do well when they are used to stock waters containing lots of forage fish in the form of bluegill sunfish (which the 'pike' don't seem to like). This may be because the naïve stockies, although they have all the red-in-tooth-and-claw equipment, are unable to catch the bluegills because they've never encountered real live prey before.

An experiment tested the effect of 'pike experience' and the 'number of prey', on the survival of the 'pike' and on the number of 'pike' managing to catch prey. Whether there were lots of prey or not many, it still didn't make much difference and the pike always managed to catch bluegill sunfish if they had to (nasty, cunning, spiky little buggers, though they are), but when they were offered alternative preferable prey of just the right size the 'pike' ate them and ignored the bluegills. When only bluegills were present the 'pike' grew very slowly and often resorted to cannibalism (*anything* obviously 'tastes' better than a bluegill). In these circumstances many of the predators died of disease and starvation. Experienced pike needed less time to catch prey and made fewer abortive strikes but they still didn't think much of bluegills. It takes pike much longer to follow, pursue, handle and swallow a spiky, deep-bodied fish like a bluegill than a nice soft, streamlined minnow. In practice, it took a pike five times as many strikes to catch a bluegill than a minnow or a shad. Even hungry pike took carp or minnows in preference to the horrible sunfish.

So pike don't like to eat bluegill sunfish, but do they really mind what their prey looks like? When they were offered normal uncoloured (brown) goldfish, odd–coloured goldfish (gold or white) and fantail goldfish the pike took them indiscriminately (in other word they didn't care much what shape or colour of prey was sliding down their throats). Now there's a surprise! It is just possible that pike are more concerned with the way potential prey moves than what it actually looks like. To bear this out, sticklebacks, with their defensive armour, move in a very unfishlike manner and pike apparently soon learn to avoid them if they have a choice.

In Swedish lakes similar comparisons of pike food preferences have been made using the more familiar rudd and perch as prey. In this case pike rarely attacked stationary fish and it was the movement of the prey that triggered an attack. When feeding in open water the pike certainly 'preferred' the soft-bodied rudd to the spiny perch. This may be partly because the rudd swim near the surface and perch are close to the lakebed – so the pike find it easier to locate rudd at distance. The more weed growth that was present, the greater was the proportion of perch devoured. It is, however, known that predators prefer fish without spines and will attack despined fish *(for example, perch with their fin spines cut off)* just as readily as soft finned ones. We're certainly not suggesting that anyone should mutilate baitfish of course. When pike were present in a water, the perch tended to avoid the weedy margins and the rudd, in contrast, to seek them out. The pike took longer to turn and swallow a perch than a rudd of similar size and rudd were much more often taken by the middle of their body, suggesting that the mid-body spines of the perch might be the most important deterrent. Is it possible that projecting, 'spiny looking' hook points could put off a pike? We don't think so – but you never know. The area just in front of the 'middle-cut' of a fish's body should be the easiest bit to grasp because it is the section that wriggles least when they are swimming. When they were seized, perch flared their sharp gill covers (they do it when you're unhooking them) and so took longer for the pike to 'turn'. Of course the spines could also damage the throat or stomach of the predator. As a matter of interest, in this study pike ate most small silver fish in May and June.

So we have established that, although they have broad tastes, pike *can* be fussy about what they eat. It is now well known that deeper-bodied crucian carp take longer for pike to turn and swallow than their slender relatives. As a result the predators tend to prefer slim crucians and will pick them out from a shoal of similar-sized fish. Something that is less often considered, in relation to visual predators like pike, is the effect of chemicals released into the water, both by the pike and by their potential prey. Crucian carp, which always tend to live in weedy areas, are certainly affected by substances emanating from pike living in the same waters. They will be less active when they are able to 'smell' pike and will also tend to spend even more time than usual in the weeds. In the absence of pike, the carp are more or less nocturnal with activity peaks before dawn and after dusk. Surprisingly, when 'pike juice' is present, the crucians are active throughout the twenty-four hours. Pike-adapted (i.e. deep-bodied) crucians are less scared by the presence of pike scent than their skinnier cousins.

As we've mentioned earlier, crucian carp change their shape to reduce the risks of being eaten by pike. What's not so well known is that other species of prey fish do something similar. The way that fish react to the presence of pike depends on their 'anti-predator strategy', in other words whether they try to bluff it out, beat a hasty retreat or head for the protection of cover when a pike is about. You might wonder whether the stress of worrying about being eaten would affect prey fish. When baby perch and roach were put in aquaria with pike, it was found that the presence of pike in the tanks had no effect on the growth of either prey species. However, as in the case of crucians, both species changed their body form when *Esox* was swimming in the tank. Just as in the case of crucians, the perch became deeper bodied, which would make them more difficult to 'mouth' than before, so that they were less likely to be attacked by smaller pike. In contrast, some of the fins of the roach changed shape and shifted their positions on the body, presumably making the fish more manoeuvrable or faster to flee the attentions of the predator. In contrast to the crucian carp, bleak show increased schooling activity (they stay closer together and are more wary) in the presence of pike 'scent' but only in the hours of daylight.

Despite the myths about fish having poor memories, there is no doubt that over time they get to know each other. It is also clear that shoaling together of baitfish is a tactic for avoiding predation. Studies with various types of minnows have shown that they shoal better and are more skilled at dodging pike if they know their shoalmates well. As a result a group consisting of 'unfamiliar' fish are more likely to be eaten than ones shoaling with their 'friends'.

We've said already that although pike will eat almost any other fish, they are less inclined to attack prickly sticklebacks, bluegills and perch. Experiments have shown that the spines do act as predator deterrents. The vulnerability of different prey fish to pike predation has been examined in detail by American scientists Mauck and Coble. The idea was to find out whether pike 'preferred ' to eat any particular species; many of the fish observed don't occur in the UK but carp, perch and pike were all used as prey. Circular plastic swimming pools, some with branches introduced to provide cover and small ponds with growths of plants were stocked with prey fish and an hour later pike were put in. The prey fish of different species were all about the same size, the idea being to see which ones the pike ate. Control ponds contained prey fish but no pike.

Of the European species present in these experiments, carp were the most popular prey, perch were middling and pike were least vulnerable. Not surprisingly injured or diseased fish were more likely to be eaten. In this case murky water made very little difference to vulnerability of prey. Like sticklebacks, catfish with spines were not a popular item of pike food. Even when pike were fed on a single species of fish (golden shiner or bluegill) for months they could not be trained (conditioned) to select that species more often than others that they naturally preferred.

In contrast to the daytime feeding pike, the walleye (like the European zander) is mainly nocturnal, feeding at night or under low light conditions. By comparing the feeding success of pike and walleye (=zander), it was possible to show that the pike do better in clear water while the walleyes, which are largely nocturnal, feed most effectively in coloured (cloudy or turbid) water conditions. The pike did not grow well in the murk, even though temperatures were almost ideal and there were stacks of prey fish to eat. This may partly explain why pike move away from the shallow water when wind 'stirs it up'.

In three Scottish lochs the pike had only a limited range of prey available. One loch contained only eels and a few trout and the other two also held perch. The 'perchless' loch was richer and had more blooms of algae and less weed growth than the other two. These gloomy conditions may have made things difficult for the pike, which had emptier stomachs and grew more slowly than those in the lochs containing perch. Interestingly, in these waters ducklings made up a fair proportion (up to 20 per cent) by weight of the food of the pike.

Having considered the evidence of what they like to eat, we are now left to decide how we will catch our pike. Of course, there are lots of different approaches ranging from feathery flies to static dead baits and from plastic plugs to rubber fish. Every pike angler will have their favourite approaches and often it is a matter of personal preference rather than what is likely to be most effective. The following pages contain accounts of what we enjoy doing and there's no doubt if you adopt the same approach you'll catch plenty of pike.

- Studies show that a young pike in its first year could each eat as many as 500–600 coarse fish fry.
- Pike tend to prefer slim crucians and will pick them out from a shoal of similar-sized fish.
- Pike anglers can damage the pike population themselves if they intentionally or accidentally kill or remove them (effectively they are 'over-fished').
- The type and size of bait used for pike makes a real difference to the size of the fish caught (generally big baits for big fish). Small baits, less than 7.5cm in length, are more likely to hook the fish in the gills and less likely to hook them in the upper jaw than larger baits.
- Deep-hooked pike of all sizes are more likely to bleed than those hooked superficially. Few pike die from the immediate effects of being caught but those that die later are likely to be the ones that bled when they were caught.

10 TALES OF PIKE FISHING

When it comes down to it, whatever the scientists say, every angler must simply do the best they can. The whole essence of fishing (at least for us) is to enjoy the sport and, hopefully, to learn something from every trip.

This chapter contains Mike's descriptions of many piking sessions by him and his friends. Over the years the tackle and tactics used for most of his pike fishing have changed dramatically, if gradually. Rods are now lightweight carbon fibre instruments capable of casting large lures or baits with accuracy and setting hooks with confidence. Modern reels are relatively cheap, and the best ones are superbly engineered and totally reliable. Instead of stretchy nylon monofilament the lines are now braided Kevlar – many times stronger for its diameter and incredibly supple. Trace wire is no longer the horrible springy, kinky material that it once was, having been replaced by a multi-stranded, stainless, plastic coated, knottable filament that may last for several fish or even several trips without a kink or fray.

Hooks are reliable, strong and often chemically sharpened. For use with live or dead baits single, debarbed, circle hooks can replace tandem barbed or semi-barbless trebles with the result that few fish are ever hooked anywhere but in the lip. The surgical hook removal operations of years gone by, involving long forceps, gags and bleeding fingers, are no longer necessary. There should be no lame excuses for fish hooked in the gut or for pike having escaped trailing lures, hooks and metres of line.

A vast range of lures is now available, but the basic types have changed little with the possible exception of the introduction of soft plastics and the increasing popularity of large jerkbaits and fly fishing methods with appropriately large flies. Despite the multiplicity of lures, large spoons are still very effective, as are soft plastics of the 'Bulldawg' type and big plugs. The latter tend to be armed with at least two trebles, which is a bit of a downer when it comes to the problem of damaged mouths and tangled landing nets. However, pike are still pike and on the whole the biggest ones will tend to fall to big dead or live baits.

Anyway, here goes with some tales of pike fishing sessions. Mike says that you should bear in mind that he is not a 'pike specialist' so there will be no week-long sessions at 'top waters' in search of monsters. If he seems to have an inordinate number of tropical holidays, you must remember that the following accounts cover several years of fishing. We start off with an offering from our pal and former colleague, that great all-round angler Stuart Clough, which fills in some of our deficiencies in the area of catching pike on the fly. Stu's contribution is all the more impressive because he has only tried this tactic a few times himself. From what he says it's clear that casting a fly is as exciting and may be as productive as any method for anglers interested in pike. Fly fishing is on the up and up these days. Anglers, probably disillusioned with fishing for stocked trout, have turned to bass and pike as worthy captures. There's no doubt in our minds that a big pike on fly tackle can make the adrenaline flow.

A modern rod armed with a decent fixed spool loaded with braid will cope with any pike that swims.

Fly Fishing for Pike, by Dr Stuart Clough

I have always felt that fly fishing in any guise is a very specialized branch of the sport of angling, which despite having being initially designed to cunningly present very lightweight 'baits' at range in very specialized circumstances, had evolved to be a fashionable technique designed to make things more challenging for those who were keen to demonstrate that they had superior skill. It should come as no surprise, given this mindset, that I initially considered fly fishing for pike as little more than a gimmick, aimed at trout anglers who wanted something to do in the winter.

I must confess that, having put my prejudice to one side, I am now a total convert. Indeed, I would now go so far as to say that in certain circumstances fly fishing for pike is *at least* as effective as lure fishing for them. It appears that there

Chew Valley reservoir – a trout fishery that now holds many large pike.

is something almost irresistibly appealing about a very slow sinking lure worked very slowly, and while some conventional lure fishing aficionados might disagree, the best way of presenting a lure of this type in this way is undoubtedly with fly gear. Add to that the exhilaration of playing a hard fighting fish on a line with no stretch and a rod that transmits far more than it absorbs, and you might start to understand the appeal. Still not convinced? Follow the advice of a former sceptic – don't knock it 'til you've tried it!

Rods, Reels and Lines

Like any other branch of the sport, it is important to have 'balanced' tackle, and the size, weight and wind resistance associated with pike flies make this arguably an even more vital consideration in pike fly fishing than in any other form of 'the noble art'. Reels are effectively just line holders, so choose one that will stand the

test of time, and provide balance to the rod. The general consensus seems to be that the best rod for the job is a 9ft, No. 9 weight, which can be matched with either a WF9F (number nine, weight forward, floating) or the equivalent intermediate or sinking line to suit conditions (and how deep you want to fish). One important additional consideration is the leader material. Twelve pound monofilament is about right for the leader but, as with every other branch of pike fishing, a wire trace is essential. That said, most of the conventional wire trace materials are not designed for the rigours of fly casting and specialist traces are the order of the day. Part wire/part braid, some of the latest hook link materials (e.g. Proleader) are incredibly flexible while retaining the pike-proof qualities of wire. While not cheap to buy, you will struggle to fish effectively without these specialist hook links, so the investment is well worthwhile.

A typical large 'Dead Budgie' pike 'fly'. These lures can be fished slowly and are attractive to pike of all sizes.

A modest Chew Valley pike taken on the fly by Dr Stuart Clough.

Casting

Casting a pike fly is, in essence, the same as casting any other fly, with an added degree of difficulty and danger related to the physical size and weight of the fly and hook. If you are used to flicking a gold head 'Czech style' for grayling on a river then double hauling a 'dead budgie' on a windswept reservoir might seem like a daunting challenge, but most competent fly casters make the switch seamlessly, given a few minutes of practice. In fact, casting distance is not the be all and end all, and targeting the right areas and adjusting the retrieve to suit the conditions are equally important considerations.

Flies

Affectionately referred to as 'dead budgies' due to their size and appearance, pike flies come in an enormous range of shapes, shades and sizes. As with lures, it is pretty well impossible to say

Stuart with a bigger fly-caught pike.

categorically which one is the 'best'. My biggest fly-caught pike (25lb) came to a small black perch pattern, while I netted a 36lb specimen for my boat partner the following day on the biggest, gaudiest fly I have ever seen. Suffice it to say, there are a number of tried and trusted patterns to start with, and if these don't do the business, persevere and try something out of the ordinary, as the next cast could produce a personal best.

Poppers

Poppers are worth a section in their own right, just because of the sheer exhilaration that results from catching pike on them, and because they can produce the goods when virtually all else fails. For some reason, pike that have retired to the cover of a dense reed bed or lily pad stand can still be encouraged to accelerate faster than Concorde to intercept a small popping surface lure in the middle of the day. Given that fly fishing usually occurs at close range, you will be startled and excited in equal measure when even a moderately sized pike goes airborne, and this technique is always worth a go, even when all else fails.

Tactics

Once the rod, reel, line and fly are selected, the speed and nature of the retrieve are essentially the main things you can vary from one cast to the next. There is no single best approach, and it all depends what the fish want on the day. A very slow 'creep' retrieve can be deadly, as can tucking the rod under your arm and 'double handing' as fast as you can. One thing is for sure, when you find some feeding fish, it soon will be clear which approach is the most effective on the day.

So, there it is, straight from the horse's mouth. If you want to find out how to cast a fly you'll have to look elsewhere but, as with all fishing, the main secret of success is to be in the right place at the right time. And now on to some of Mike's pike fishing experiences.

What a fish! Dr Alastair Stephen's 36lb fish caught on fly gear.

Happy New Year

Over Christmas I went pike fishing a few times in my local river. It was often frosty and cold but I was encouraged by my pal Nigel who had not fished for pike before and was very enthusiastic to catch his first. I knew that Nigel had done a fair bit of spinning in the sea, so on our first trip we decided to use wobbled dead baits. When you get down to it there is not much difference between spinning for pike and spinning for bass and by keeping on the move I thought

it was likely to be warmer and more comfortable (for us, not the pike) than using static dead baits.

I sometimes fix a small wine-bottle cork (slit with a razor blade) to the line above my wire trace. This easily adjustable float has the benefits of fixing the depth at which the bait is fished, showing the position of the bait and acting as a bite indicator. The bait is then cast into likely places (often slack areas with overhead or underwater cover) and twitched slowly back. We were both using conventional C-hooks.

A wine-bottle cork slit with a razor blade makes a good 'indicator'.

Nigel's second ever pike – not a bad way to start a 'piking career'.

Nigel's first cast resulted in a bite from a fish of five or six pounds, which whipped the cork under. Although I could see from his reactions that Nigel was 'hooked', unfortunately the fish wasn't and after a few seconds it came unstuck. Unusually the pike refused to bite again and we moved on to another spot. The fishing was slow that afternoon and, apart from a decent fish that took my wobbled dace, we had no other bites.

On our second trip Nigel already had the hang of things and it was not long until his first fish was on the bank – probably the one he had lost on the previous session. I had one (a bit smaller) from the opposite bank and then Nigel landed a beautiful fifteen-pounder. Meanwhile a much bigger fish had a go at my bait but managed to avoid the hook. The large fish led a charmed life and each of us contrived to miss a couple of takes from it. By now we were out of bait so we packed in and left 'Houdini' for a future occasion.

Spinning rod, fixed spool reel and braided line – Mike uses much the same gear for bass fishing as for piking.

The Transition

It is that time of year (Novemberish) when I usually change the bulk of my fishing from salt to freshwater. The writing was on the wall when my last two bass spinning trips were 'blown off' – the first by winds so strong that they threatened to blow me into the sea and the second by seas so rough that I could not get to the rocks I wanted to fish off. Of course, the bass are probably still there and by careful choice of times and places I expect I shall be able to catch a few more but it is time to consider other possibilities.

Following the first dud trip, I took the lure off the line, tied on a size eight carp hook and went carp fishing for a couple of hours. I lost two good fish (hooks popped out!) on freelined cubes of luncheon meat and landed one six-pounder on a couple of Chum Mixers. I saw the latter fish take a few free offerings before casting the bait to it.

After my second abortive bassing session, I decided to have an afternoon spinning for pike in my local river. I used the same reel and braided line (with the addition of a wire trace) that I use for bass, but replaced the rod with a heavier (3lb TC) version to allow for setting the larger hooks on my big pike spoon.

The river was gin-clear and still full of streamer weed in the shallower stretches of water. I started just upstream of the weir pool and second cast lobbed the spoon onto the far bank, where it stuck in the grass. I walked back to the weir, over the bridge, up the south bank and retrieved the spoon before returning to my rod. Next cast a pike slashed at the spoon twice. The second time it actually bumped it and made the hooks jangle audibly against the metal of the lure. I cast again and this time I saw the

Again the bass/pike tackle is more than adequate for most carp.

fish sweep past the spoon as it struck – the pike was obviously determined to have its meal. Next cast it missed again and then, as I was about to lift the lure out, it grabbed it and was hooked just under the chin.

I landed the pike (about 5lb) took a photograph, returned it and continued fishing. Ten minutes later a larger pike came at the spoon from under a fallen tree, missed and would not come back (I should have had a dead bait in the bag; it usually helps to tempt reluctant fish). Another ten minutes – I had crossed over and was on my way back down the south bank – and I caught another small fish, which was hooked first time, landed, photographed and returned.

A good first session of the winter! Just downstream of the weir pool, I decided to have a last chuck into a little weedy bay. I could see the big spoon slowly wobbling as I held it in the gentle flow just outside a dense raft of surface weed.

A smallish pike taken on a spoon.

A bigger pike taken on the same spoon. These lures are extremely effective and very versatile.

Suddenly it was in the jaws of a pike and I struck sharply to fix the hooks. This was a much better fish and battled hard for the best part of five minutes before I could slide it into the edge and lift it out onto the wet grass. Eighteen pounds and well hooked just in front of the scissors. I might have another go tomorrow!

Taken on the Flood

Rain, rain, rain! It seems to have done little else for months. Even here in Dorset, where much

of the river water is filtered by massive layers of chalk, the water colours up on floods. The *first* autumn floods are by far the worst from this point of view because all the accumulated rubbish and sediment of the summer is washed out at this time, together with the runoff from farmland, quarries, roads and construction sites. As winter progresses, the amount of sediment disturbed by the floods decreases and, typically, as the water rises to its peak it is already well on the way to clearing. Experience shows that if the water is reasonably clear there is a fair chance of a pike.

With this in mind I went out last Friday for

The river can be 'bank high' but clear after a flood.

an hour's spinning just to see what was about. As I waded, thigh-deep in floodwater, across the field towards the river, I noticed that there were a few people duck-shooting so I decided to give them as much space as I could, for the benefit of my own safety as well as their sport. Two of them were already standing on the bank of the river just where I had intended fishing.

My lure was a big silver spoon with an outsize treble (I have flattened the barbs and sharpened the points). The large hook wags back and forth making the lure (I think) look very like a slowly swimming fish. There were very few places where it seemed worth having a cast and I moved along the flooded riverbanks looking for little slacks or pools sheltered from the main flow. Even the best-looking places often swirled and boiled every few minutes as some slight shift in the pattern of the currents swept in an eddy from the main river channel.

Nigel piking in flood conditions. Only the reeds show where the river starts and the field ends.

After half-an-hour with no sign of a fish I noticed that the shooters had left the spot where I wanted to fish so I made my way slowly towards it. My favoured place was the end of a reedy oxbow and, sure enough, the water was calm and clear. I swung the spoon out to the edge of the reeds and as it hit the water I began to retrieve. The pike must have been lying by my bank because as the spoon reached my feet there was a great splash and a swirl. The rod tip yanked down and I was well into a decent fish.

Before long the fish was beached and the hook more or less fell out as I slackened the line. By now it was pretty gloomy and yet another heavy shower was well underway. I returned the fish and after a few words with the soaking wet shooters I packed in and went home. Definitely better than watching the telly!

A nice pike strikes at the wobbling spoon and is hooked. This is the real excitement of pike fishing for us.

Joe's First Pike

The floods I mentioned earlier were by now subsiding. While the water was still very high, I tried another short session spinning with my big spoon. It was almost impossible to find a suitable spot in the main river so I decided to have a go in a slack mill head. There were no real features and the water was quite deep (about 2.5m), but because it was clear I was confident that any pike present would be able to see the lure. On about the tenth cast I hit a fish which rushed about a bit before it was landed. As I unhooked it, the edge of the gill cover slit my finger open – the pike's revenge!

A few days later I went fishing again with my pal Nigel and his son Joe. Joe is a very keen angler but had never caught a pike so we were

Joe's first pike slides towards the net. What a feeling!

quite keen for him to get one. The first two or three spots seemed to be devoid of fish, so we decided to walk upstream until we found a good place. Sure enough, after plodding through mud and water for five minutes we saw a beautiful slack on our bank – deep and weedy, with hardly any flow at all. Ideal! Joe dropped his bait, suspended under a bottle cork, into the edge and within a minute a good pike slashed at it right on the surface. Surprised by the speed of the attack, Joe jerked the bait away from the fish and it missed it.

Within seconds of returning the bait to the water, the pike had it again and the reel screeched as the fish took off downstream. The pike fought hard and at one point dived into a solid bed of last year's milfoil, but Joe was not about to lose his first ever pike. He shifted down the bank and eased the fish out of its hidey-hole before playing it to the net. After the fish was unhooked, it weighed in at

12lb and Joe had his picture taken before putting his fish back in the river. Fantastic!

Failing to Catch Perch

As Christmas approaches the chances to go fishing seem to become progressively less, nevertheless I decided to try and catch some dace from a local stream. I went with my son Richard who was with us for the day. It had been quite frosty on the previous night and at first things were quite slow. We had chosen to fish in a small hatch pool with ledgered maggots, but bites were thin on the ground. After a bite of lunch, the sun had come out and we felt more hopeful. Sure enough this time the fish were biting and we landed a couple of dozen small dace, roach, gudgeon and grayling, plus several big fat minnows.

A chubby little gudgeon.

A small grayling landed by Mike in his festive hat.

On the following day I went over to the River Stour with my friend Keith Starks and we both spun spoons, plugs and spinners for a couple of hours without success. As we fished we saw several coarse anglers on the far bank catching small roach and one chap who was quiver-tipping had a decent perch of perhaps a pound.

A couple of days later, as the weather warmed up, I was fired with enthusiasm and decided to try for perch where I had seen the fish caught. I wanted to catch big fish if possible, so small live baits were the order of the day. I had no trouble catching half a dozen small roach and dace, and I rigged simple cork float, on six-pound braid, above a light, knottable wire trace and single hook on which to lip-hook my baits. The first bite came about five seconds after I dropped the bait into the water (just where I'd seen the perch landed). Clearly it was not a perch (unless it was the biggest ever) and I was glad I'd opted for

A modest pike taken while fishing for perch. The knottable wire trace is essential in case of pike.

the wire next to the hook. As luck would have it, the pike came unstuck after a short fight. In the next half hour I had two more pike, both of six or seven pounds, but not a sign of a perch. I released the spare baits and went home, intending have another go before Christmas if I could.

End of Season Pike

I decided to have one final go at the pike in the River Frome before the end of the season. I only had a couple of smallish baits, so I was not too optimistic and for the best part of an hour there was no sign of anything. Anyway, it was a lovely afternoon with the sun shining and the river in perfect condition at last, so I pressed on. Just downstream of a deep, fast-flowing run was a little slack on my bank. The area of slow flow was no more than a metre wide and only a couple of metres long. Along the edge was a small patch of floating vegetation – just the spot for a pike to lurk in.

I dropped the bait into the slack and let it swing slowly round, suspended only about half a metre under the cork float. After a couple of circuits, I began to lift the bait out so as to swing it back into the upstream end of the slack. As the bait emerged from the water, it was followed by a 'Polaris' pike that missed, crashed back in and soaked me with spray. I plopped the bait back in, close to where the pike was last seen and waited. The time seemed to drag but it can't have been much more than a minute before the float submerged steadily.

I tightened and felt a heavy resistance. The pike moved out into the flow. I held the rod in my right hand and leaned back to pick up my little camera (always at the ready) with my left. The line began to rise in the water so I pointed the lens at where I thought the fish was and pressed the shutter – too late! It's never easy to fish and photograph at the same time.

When the pike was landed it proved to be a

Pike do sometimes provide exciting 'surface action', but it's rare to have the camera ready (particularly if you're alone).

Careful Nige! Precariously poised on the bank, Nigel puts a bit of pressure on a hooked fish.

12lb female in good condition. I took a couple of pictures, unhooked it and returned it. On my way back to the car I decided to have a go in a small, overgrown ditch. Sure enough, within minutes of starting I had another bite and landed a fish of about 3lb, again hooked neatly in the lip. Good enough for my last afternoon's piking before leaving for Australia. Hopefully when I got back at the beginning of April, I would have some different pictures for the website.

Back to the Pike!

I'd been on holiday to Tobago. It is always a bit of a wrench returning from temperatures of 32°C and catching bonefish in tropical seas, to cold muddy riverbanks and pike fishing. However, it's always a pleasure to go fishing with my pal Nigel and I needed no second bidding to give the pike a try.

To be honest, the river had been a bit grim

recently with sudden yo-yo changes in temperature seeming to put the fish off. However, the day dawned bright and clear and we had decided to try the afternoon, giving the water a chance to warm up a bit. A couple of days earlier a few of my friends had been piking in the same river and had struggled to catch anything – finishing up with a two-pounder and a five-pounder after a long session, so we were not too optimistic.

When we arrived the river was high and a bit coloured, not the ideal conditions for pike fishing. Anyway, we tackled up and began to trot our natural baits, suspended under small floats, round the likely spots. There were very few decent slacks in the high flow conditions and the first couple of places that we tried, although they looked pretty good in the circumstances, did not produce so much as a sniff. We moved on to try the prime place – a large oxbow – with

With the bait still on the hook the pike is tired now.

Landed! Time to get the hook out and put the fish back.

me on one side of the slack and Nigel round at the other side.

Before long I heard a great crash from Nigel's stance and when I asked if he had a fish he told me that a good pike had lunged and splashed at the bait just by his feet. I watched as he put on a smaller bait and began to fish again. We were pretty confident that the fish would have another go but it must have been ten minutes before I saw him strike. By the time I plodded round to where he was standing, the fish was still rushing about and taking line. I grabbed the camera and walked about taking a few pictures and chuckling as the pike made run after run and as Nige slipped and slithered about in the mud. Eventually he landed, unhooked, weighed and returned the fish – a 16lb beauty. We had no more bites.

A couple of days later I had a fourteen-pounder, from another slack a couple of miles

'How'm I going to get this one out?' Nigel plays a decent fish hooked from a rickety bridge.

upstream, which fought just as well as Nigel's fish. Fantastic! There's more to fishing than sunshine and blue seas!

Pike Fishing

The weather improved a lot over a couple of weeks. At last the rain stopped, more or less, the rivers went back between their banks and

the temperatures rose above freezing point. For some reason (unknown to me) as time went on the coarse fish became more and more reluctant to bite, so obtaining pike baits became quite difficult.

The bait problem, at first, made me resort to spinning with a big spoon. In my book this is very much a 'third best' method from the point of view of attracting the best pike, but at least it is pretty mobile and allows you to cover lots of water that would, otherwise, never be fished.

Just like the bait fishing, I struggled to get a bite but eventually persistence paid off and a nice fish took the spoon almost under my feet (as a matter of interest I regard 'struggling' as an hour or more with no sign of a fish). In fact the fish missed at its first attempt and I saw it lunge past the lure in only about two feet of water. Experience has shown that, in these circumstances (if you have no natural bait) the best thing to do is (1) wait a minute, (2) cast well away from the fish, and (3) spin the lure back towards the pike's lie. Sure enough the strategy worked so as the spoon reached the critical point I saw a green flash and felt a heavy, dragging weight on the line. The fish, about 10lb, did not put up much of a struggle and was soon landed.

Encouraged by my catch, I decided to have another go the following weekend. Nigel and his son Joe came with me and after (with some difficulty) obtaining a few baits, we tried the stretch that I had fished with my spoon. Joe was the first in action and, before Nigel or myself had our tackle in the water he called out that he had a pike on. The fish proved to be a good one (pushing 20lb) but after half-a-minute of give and take the hook came free. Despite Joe's best efforts, two more takes from the same fish proved abortive so we moved on.

To cut a long story short, Joe had two more fish, including a nice, double-figure one, and Nigel also had a couple, one hooked from a stance on an old bridge – I had nothing on the spoon. Not bad for a couple of hour's fishing, but the big one's still there – waiting to be caught!

Piking

The big pike that we missed on my last trip to the river had fired my enthusiasm. I waited a few days until conditions looked good and set off for another attempt. I had one good-sized bait and three or four smaller ones so, ever optimistic, I put the big one on the hook and went straight to the place where the big fish had failed to take my bait. The rig was simple – a single J-hook (I always use circle hooks now) on 20lb wire and a cork with a slit in it for a float. I fished the pool for ten minutes with no sign of life and just as I approached the last bit of slack at the upstream end, a good fish (I couldn't tell if it was the one I was after) lunged out at the bait and missed. I waited with my heart in my mouth for it to have another go and, just as I was thinking it was not coming back, the float submerged with hardly a ripple. I raised the rod and could feel the weight of the pike on the end so I took in a couple of turns of line and struck. The hook came back baitless. I could have wept. I tried again with one of the smaller baits but no joy so it will have to wait a bit longer before I have another go.

Disappointed, I set off for the next pool, probably the best on the stretch, and floated a 15cm bait all round the deep slow water on the outside of the bend for ten minutes or so – nothing! I walked round to the other side of the pool and cast the bait 20m across into the shallow slack on the inside of the same bend. I began a slow retrieve and after about ten seconds the float went under with a plop and there was a tell-tale swirl just where it had disappeared. Tighten, strike and it was on. The pike went berserk, splashing, lunging out of the water and rushing about the pool and generally causing chaos before I managed to land it. It was beautifully hooked in the scissors, so I took a few pictures and slid the fish back.

There was still a big area of slack unfished, so I decided to try again in the same spot. Sure enough, a couple of minutes later, as I was retrieving the bait slowly, there was a great splash and a glimpse of broad green back as another fish took the bait. Again I tightened and struck to feel a much heavier weight. This one did not show itself, but simply bored about into the deeper water. It was some time before the cork appeared above the surface and even longer before I had a good sight of the fish – a beauty, again hooked in the corner of the mouth. I landed it on the soft, wet, grassy bank, photographed it, weighed it and returned it – just under 19lb.

I put on my last bait and moved up to the next pool, but after a couple of casts the bait fell off and I packed in and went home. A good session, even if I did not catch the big fish.

A decent pike on bait and there's that silly hat again; amazingly it doesn't seem to deter the pike!

Fair-Weather Fisherman

Despite the fact that the water companies are moaning about a drought situation, the recent rain has certainly curtailed my fishing. It's not that I mind fishing in the rain and I will even put up with the rain starting before I tackle up. However, the thing I can't abide is my gear getting soaked. I have never found a totally waterproof bag or haversack to carry my stuff in. It seems to me that it is a real pain trying to dry off, not only the bag itself, but the spare spools, containers of hooks, etc. and above all the cameras in their own little padded bag. I'm sure that the hiking and cycling fraternity have waterproof covers for their back-packs. I must try to find one.

Anyway, I got up early (twice) last weekend to go down to the coast. On both occasions I dressed and got the tackle together before opening the door to find that it was already pouring down. Both times I chickened out and stayed in.

Of course the sequel to the rain was that the river came up in flood and coloured up badly, so it was not until mid-week that I decided it was worth a go. I opted to ledger for grayling. With the best part of a pint of maggots, I set off for the river. Now I'm not the world's greatest coarse angler but I can usually catch something

so, after I had tried two or three decent glides without a sniff, I was beginning to get despondent. I decided to try a place where the river ran down the far bank in a fast, shallow riffle. On my bank was a slack about half a metre deep. By casting my shot ledger over into the fast flow, I could let it swing across and settle in the slack. I chucked in a handful of maggots and started to fish. Within minutes I had a good bite and landed a grayling, and then next cast I had

Sploosh!!!!

another. The third bite was missed and then there were no more. My pal Adrian says that I should use a swim feeder and I'm sure he's right but they always seem such clumsy great things to me. I do have such a gadget in the bag so perhaps I should have tried it.

Typically I was not satisfied with catching little fish, so I decided to have an hour or so after pike. First cast the cork zipped under and a fifteen-pounder roared away across the pool. It put up a fantastic show of jumps and rolls before it was banked. The next four spots produced another three pike, none as big as the first. I have to say that I always feel more at home when I'm after big, predatory fish, I suppose it's just the way I am, but I must have another go for the grayling soon.

Joe's Best Pike Yet

One weekend I went out fishing with Nigel and Joe. The idea was to fish for grayling and dace at first and then to have a go for a pike. The fact is that only Nigel and Joe fished because I had injured my back and was trying to nurse it back to health. Anyway, I decided not to fish but to take my little camera and follow the lads about as they caught fish. A bit frustrating, but there we are!

We started off by trying to catch some grayling, dace or roach. Both Nigel and Joe were float fishing with maggots as bait and within a few minutes of starting Nigel landed a roach of a few ounces so it was looking good. In fact the catch was a bit of a red herring as, after that, things were distinctly slow. Eventually Nigel had a grayling a bit bigger than the roach and after a couple of moves Joe landed another reasonable grayling.

By now the afternoon was wearing on and it was time to try piking. We slung the gear into the cars and drove a mile or so to another stretch where there were several good pools and where we had seen a very big fish a week or so before. Despite the conditions looking good, the pike were a bit on the slow side and for half-an-hour there was no sign of life. Eventually I walked with Joe to the spot where I had seen the large fish previously. He drifted his bait round

the big eddy and eventually, as it crossed a bankside bay, the float shot away. Not wanting to risk deep hooking (although it rarely happens with the circle hooks we were using) Joe tightened and the rod bent to a decent pike before springing back as the bait was neatly removed from the hook.

With only one smallish bait left, Joe baited up and tried again. We thought that there was a good chance that the pike would have another go if we could locate it. There was no sign of life in the bay where the first take occurred, so the bait was allowed to drift round the pool. Eventually after about ten minutes of trying, Joe plopped the bait just up current of where the pike had been lost. Within a few seconds the float submerged sharply. This time there was no mistake and the pike, nicely hooked in the jaw, rushed around the pool. When we landed the pike it was not the monster but a cracking fish of 14lb – Joe's best yet.

Mike's Pike

Once again the weather had been mixed. Whenever I felt like going fishing it seemed to rain heavily the day before. Now my local river reaches peak flood conditions in about twenty-four hours, so piking is usually out of the question for a couple of days. Time after time the depressions, with their accompanying rain, seemed to swing across at just the wrong intervals.

Anyway, one weekend there was a brief window in the bad weather so when Nigel rang and offered to help me with a bit of bank clearance I was dead keen to get out. Of course, in addition to the axe and the loppers we both took rods and it was not long (as soon as we had trimmed a few thorn bushes) before we were into some decent dace on float-fished maggots. One or two of the dace were a good size so we were well pleased with our start.

We trudged upstream with the pike gear and I was interested to try out my new float consisting of a post-Christmas, synthetic 'cork' (slit, as usual, with a razor blade) from a wine bottle. My 'cork' seemed to grip the line very well but Nigel said that he had tried cutting some of

I'm sure that Nigel agreed a bit of bank trimming was probably in order.

these plastic 'corks' and the slits just opened out. Presumably there must be different types of plastic 'cork' in use? Further investigation is needed. Anyway, I dropped my bait in by the bank and the float shot away before Nigel had managed to bait up. I must have plonked it right on the pike's nose. After a fair old struggle I landed a lovely sixteen-pounder. We did a bit more fishing and some more bank trimming, but the only other fishy action was a pike of

10–12lb that managed to evade both our hooks in succession.

A Good Variety

Last weekend I went fishing with Joe and Nigel again. The river was still high and had a bit of colour but the weather was a good bit milder even though there was a chilly wind blowing.

A fair sized pike is always pleasing.

A parr. These greedy little fish can be a nuisance when you're trying to catch coarse fish on maggots.

When I arrived, the other two were already fishing. They were sharing a float rod and fishing a shallow glide in the little mill stream. I was just in time to see Joe return a reasonable grayling and, it seemed, they had already landed quite a few of these lovely fish. Needless to say, my presence put the damper on the fish and all they caught after I got there was a salmon parr – still it was encouraging.

We shifted upstream to a small weir pool with a strong flow down the middle. Joe fished the right hand side and Nigel the left while I watched and took a few pictures. The fish weren't exactly mad-on, but they came steadily – dace, roach, trout, gudgeon, grayling, salmon parr and even a perch. Enough variety to keep everyone occupied. For some reason Nigel dropped loads of fish after a second or two on the hook. I guess it must have been the way the fish moved in the current that was dislodging the barbless hook from their mouths; even so, he caught plenty.

When the fishing slowed down a bit, we decided to have an hour after pike in the main river. Despite walking for a couple of miles there were very few fishable spots. The high water had resulted in most of the pikey places being very turbulent and even in the slacks we found there was nothing doing. Eventually Joe had a reasonable pike from the end of a ditch where the water was virtually still and a bit clearer than in the main river. Eight species in a short afternoon – excellent.

Back Soon!

My last fishing trip was when I went to the river with my friend Jon Hulland. Jon is one of the keen bass anglers who I meet sometimes when I'm down at the coast, and when I asked him if he fancied a few hours after pike he jumped at the chance. To tell the truth, the conditions were pretty poor. In fact for the previous two weeks I'd put off the trip time and again because of the state of the river. As soon as it looked as if we might get two days without much rain we decided to give it a try. The river was bank-high but on the credit side it was beginning to clear. I had a few baits so we went straight to the river. After the first couple of pools the writing was on the wall – this was not a good day for piking.

I decided to shift to another stretch so we jumped in the cars and drove downstream. After a hike across the fields we reached a nice pool with a back eddy. Even in the high water it looked quite 'pikey' so out went the floats. After a few minutes Jon called to let me know that he had a fish on. The pike put up a spirited resistance and I was able to take a couple of pictures. After we had returned Jon's fish we tried a few more spots but – nothing! We had to pack in fairly early because we both had appointments in mid-afternoon. Hopefully next time the fish will be more cooperative.

Piking Again

My first trip out since I got back from Tobago was last Saturday. I rang Nigel and we elected to have a session piking. It was a cold bright after-noon and we met at one o'clock to fish on a local stretch of the River Frome. We actually started fishing at about one-thirty, having decided to concentrate on the slacks and ditches where the pike should be starting to gather prior to spawning. In the first ditch a small fish (5–6lb) attacked my bait, but I missed it and we decided to leave it and try the next pool. Nothing there so we moved on to a third spot. After a few minutes there was a mighty swirl as Nigel was about to lift his bait from the water. He tightened and the pike was firmly hooked. It put up a fine battle before I was able to net it and it weighed in at 19¾lb. What a start!

In the next ditch it was only seconds before my float shot away as another decent fish hooked itself. I held it hard to avoid submerged scaffolding and willow trees. This one weighed almost 17lb – another beauty. At the end of the same ditch Nigel had his second – this time a smaller fish of 6–7lb. We were well chuffed.

We tramped back up the other bank and after finding nothing in the next pool we had a cast into a dead slack behind a fallen tree covered in a mass of honeysuckle. A fish slashed at my bait right in among the submerged twigs and I commented to Nigel that I did not fancy my chance of landing it. A couple of minutes later the fish had another go and to my amazement it swam out of its lair with the bait in its mouth. I tightened and found myself attached to yet another good fish. It pulled hard, but I was able to keep it out of the tree and before long Nigel netted it for me. Just over 21lb. We finished the day off with a fish of 7–8lb landed by Nigel – it was four o'clock; almost worth coming back to the cold of the UK for a session like that.

Ben's Fishing Trips

I have a number of grandchildren and they all enjoy fishing trips. Over the last couple of weeks I have spent some time with Ben, who's seven years old, and of course we *had* to go fishing.

Our first trip was after pike so I rigged him up with a cork for a float and a debarbed single hook on a short wire trace. The bait had only been in the water for minutes when away went the cork and Ben was in! The fish pulled like

A nice fish from a flooded ditch on one of our better days.

mad and to be honest, for a while, there was not much that Ben could do with it. I told him that whatever he did he must 'Hang on to the rod!' – and he did just that. Eventually the pike tired and we were able to land it and take a picture, although he was reluctant to pick up the big, lively, toothy fish. At the next spot that we tried he was into another pike within seconds. This one came unstuck when he gave it a bit of slack, but five minutes later it took again and this time was landed. Excellent!

When we discarded the leftover baits from our piking, we had noticed a few eels showing interest in the dead fish. I suggested an eel fishing session and Ben was really keen. The following week his dad, Marc, brought him over one evening and we set off after the eels. First we had to catch some bait, so I set Ben

up with an old float rod and a few maggots. It was not long before he landed the first minnow and then the fish came thick and fast. In addition to the minnows, he caught salmon and trout parr (returned), gudgeon, dace and a small roach – all his own work. Later, with a bit of help from dad, he managed a couple of half-decent eels. Again he was a bit reluctant to get hold of the eels (who isn't?) but held one up for a picture. The eels were returned alive and well and I was plastered in slime (there must be a commercial use for eel slime!). Ben had really enjoyed his trip, particularly the float fishing session for small fish. Grandad (and dad) probably enjoyed it almost as much as he did. It really took me back a long time to when I first fished for little perch and roach – wonderful!

Young Ben pleased with a dace . . .

. . . and with a roach.

Sea Trout?

Last October I did very well with big sea trout on my local river so I decided to give it another go this month. There had been a lot of rain recently, so on the appointed Tuesday, I found the water high and coloured and did not bother to cast a line. The following day I returned for another go. I clipped on a J9F Rapala (with a little 15lb wire trace in case of pike) and began to fish. I cast across and let the plug swing back to my side, working in the current. In two hours I had four bites. The first was a definite sea trout of 2–3lb and came unstuck almost straight away. The second was a much larger fish that took the lure under a bridge; I saw it but again it came unstuck. The third one felt like a crocodile but once more it came off (by now I was beginning to wonder what was wrong with the lure). The fourth take I landed, but was disappointed to find that it was a 'red' salmon and had to go straight back.

Two days later I went again to find that the river level was about the same, but much of the colour had cleared. Again I used the J9, which fished just above the weed even in the shallowest parts of the river. I fished a stretch downstream of where I had previously tried and before long I was into a reasonable trout which, when landed, weighed 3½lb. Soon afterwards I had another, smaller trout and I was thinking about packing in. I decided to have a last cast across the shallows and walked downstream a couple of metres. As I did so I saw a bow wave move away

from the bank and thought, 'That's my chance blown!' Anyway I cast across and reeled in, just for amusement. As the little plug reached my side of the river a green torpedo lunged after it with breathtaking speed, grabbed the plug and streaked off downstream. The pike (about 6lb) put up a spirited battle before I was able to slide it into the bank, unhook and release it – a good end to two enjoyable short sessions.

Spoon-Fed

I do enjoy pike fishing! When I fish the river my favourite lure is still a large silver spoon. I tend to watch it wobble along in the clear water and often see all the action as a fish strikes. Anyway, when I decided to have a session last Thursday I clipped on the old faithful. My spoon has a pretty large hook and had not been used for quite a time so the first thing I did was sharpen it. The hooks were razor sharp – believe me.

On my third cast I hooked a pike, which shot away across the river and made a couple of decent runs before I was able to land it. Ten minutes later I had another fish – a bit bigger at about 8lb. After returning the second fish, I walked on down and cast again. Zap! It was taken by a big trout, which characteristically splashed about on the surface. It was the close season so I unhooked the trout, about 6lb, in the water and released it. Not long after the trout, I had another pike of similar size to the second. It was nearly time to pack in, so I decided to try one more spot before going home. I cast across a wide pool and retrieved the spoon. As it approached the rod tip, I looked down and saw a long green shape following – a big pike, pushing 30lb I estimated. It refused to take the spoon so, after a couple more casts with no sign, I left it, vowing to return.

The following day I went up to Bristol to help my pal Steve edit our bass video. It was late at night before I returned so no fishing that day. The next day was Saturday and we went shopping in the morning. That afternoon my wife, Lilian, went into work so I decided to have an hour after the big pike I had seen.

At the river my first job was to catch a natural bait. Within five minutes I had two dace and I set off for 'the pike pool'. I was using a circle hook on a soft wire trace and half a wine-bottle cork for a float. The bait drifted round the pool for about five minutes with no sign of life, so I

swung it out into the middle so as to fish over a shallow sand bank in the centre of the slack area. After two minutes there was a mighty swirl and the float disappeared. I let the fish take three or four metres of line and tightened – what a struggle! It was obviously the pike that had refused my spoon a couple of days earlier and it must have been five minutes before I was able to lift it from the water. 26lb (just slightly disappointing – it looked considerably bigger as it followed the spoon). A little later I had a second fish of about 9lb from another pool and that was that. Both fish were beautifully hooked round the maxillary bone. Circle hooks are wonderful!

Pike Again

My pike fishing season had started very well this year. Following the twenty-six-pounder the

Why does Mike look so miserable? It's a good pike!

other week I tried a different stretch of river – again using my big silver spoon. First cast across a shallow slack, there was a fierce take and a mighty boil as a good fish grabbed the lure. Typically the pike fought like stink with one powerful run after another. As the fish battled, I was trying to get my bag off my back and to extract the camera out of its case using only my left hand. Far from easy! I knew that the fish was a decent size right from the word go, but it seemed to be well hooked so I was in no hurry to land it. Eventually I was able to slide the pike ashore onto a mass of weed in the water margin – 16lb. Excellent!

Over the next hour I had three more fish come at the spoon – none of them managed to get hold of it, but I was not too bothered after having landed the first one. All three were smaller than the one I caught and they simply missed the lure, probably because I was fishing it with a slight sink-and-draw movement. Even though I know that pike usually have another go I did not persist after missing them but tried somewhere else. Anyway, I was well pleased with the session.

A few days later I tried yet another stretch, this time using bait. Again, first cast I saw a slight swirl near the float (my old wine-bottle cork) so I knew that there was a fish close by. I persisted in the same spot for about five minutes (a hell of a long time for me) before a long green shape slid out of the reeds and engulfed the bait in a leisurely fashion. This one took a while to wake up but when it did it shot off upstream into a strong flow before turning back down and rushing past me. I was on a high bank so the net was essential to get this one out – just over 20lb. Fantastic! Although the pike seemed to be in good condition, it had a growth on its mouth and a bit of a tatty tail – I recognized it as one caught by Joe a year ago. I fished on for another hour or so but this time there were no more bites. Funny things, pike!

They're Off!

One Sunday I went fishing with my pals Nigel and Joe. We were hoping to catch pike and/ or grayling from the river. At first we all went after pike using floats and fish baits. It was only minutes after we started that Nigel had a run. He leaned into the fish and it seemed to be well, on but after ten or fifteen seconds of tussle it came unstuck. Unusual! Nigel dropped another bait into the swim and the scenario was repeated just as before. Amazing! A few minutes later I crossed over to a pool on the opposite bank. Seconds after my bait hit the water it was taken, the float shot away and – you've guessed it – I played the fish for a while and before I had seen it – it came off. *Small fish!* I thought. It was at least five minutes before I had another take and this time I saw the fish sweep out and grab the bait; it was 10–12lb. Yet again I played the pike for a while and eventually it managed to unhook itself. Sheer incompetence, you might well think. Joe came across and joined me so I suggested that he tried for the pike. He had a run and this time the fish seemed well-hooked, so I picked up the net and prepared to land it – again it shed the hook and escaped.

By this time paranoia was setting in. The hooks were sharp, the method was no different to what we normally do, but the fish were getting away. At pools further downstream Nigel and I lost another pike and still further down Joe lost his second one. This was ridiculous. Joe continued fishing for pike, while Nigel and I switched to the grayling tackle. This proved more difficult – we couldn't buy a bite. Eventually, after feeding almost half a pint of maggots into a swim I managed to land a grayling – success at last.

All three of us reverted to piking and I took Joe over to the opposite bank again to try a big slack on the inside of the bend. I left my rod on the bank and took the camera with me, hopeful that Joe might tempt a decent fish. He drifted his bait round the shallow slack on the inside of the bend with no sign of a bite so I suggested that he tried the still water close to the bankside reeds. Within seconds there was an almighty splash and the rod was almost pulled from his grasp. The pike fought like the devil and I managed to get a few pictures as he was playing it. The first time it came to the net Joe missed it, but the second time it was just sliding over the rim when the rod suddenly straightened, the fish gave a swirl and it was gone. We were gutted.

Nigel firmly hooked into a fish on the Frome!

It's off! Occasionally pike just seem fated to escape.

When we looked it was clear that the wire had parted close to the hook – disaster. We had seen that the circle hook was only lightly in the fish's scissors and the barb was flat so no doubt it shed it quickly. The fish was well into the teens of pounds – probably Joe's best at that point so it was doubly disappointing. Before we packed in, Nigel landed the pike that he had hooked first cast of the session, but all in all it was a chronicle of losses. That's fishing!

More Pike

I am not a great lure collector. In fact, I only use a very small range of lure types but occasionally I acquire something new to tie on the end of the line as a gift or a swap or even (perish the thought) as a purchase. Just before we went to Ireland in November I was given one of those odd, fish-shaped gadgets that the anglers in the USA seem to love so dearly. The line attaches to a ring about one-third of the way back from the lure's nose and it has two trebles dangling underneath. It is a sinker with no diving vane and a trial in a local ditch showed that it vibrates like hell as you retrieve. I was intrigued and having decided that it had potential I tried the lure for bass and caught a couple of decent ones. Very good!

Last week I went piking and after flogging away fruitlessly with my favourite spoon I eventually decided to try a change. The new 'vibrator' was in my box so on it went. The lure was much too small for pike in my judgement, but it did have a good action and appearance. First cast, as the lure reached a point under the rod tip, there was a swirl and I hooked a 2lb pike. I moved to a weir pool and had a few more casts. It was almost time for me to go home when I cast right up under the sill. Wallop – another pike about three times the size of the first. I have now classified the vibrating lure, rightly or wrongly, as a 'small pike' lure along with Mepps, small plugs, Tobys, etc.

This week seven-year-old Ben came to visit for a couple of days. His first words were, 'When can we go fishing, Grandad?' That afternoon we went up the river. First we fished for dace, but after he had caught a few he was

No picture of his twenty-seven, but this is Ben's twenty-two-pounder – his third twenty-plus!

wanting something bigger. I asked if he fancied pike fishing and he needed no second bidding. We walked on down to the pool where I had caught my twenty-six-pounder a few weeks back. Ben's rod was fitted up with braid, a wire trace with a circle hook and half a wine-bottle cork for a float. He lobbed it into the pool and waited for a few minutes as it drifted round. It is a large pool and it took some time for the float to work its way into the middle of the eddy but, as it did so, there was a huge swirl just by the float. Ben yanked with surprise and the pike missed the bait. I told him to lob it back out and try again. It was five minutes (more like five days for a seven-year-old, believe me) before the float whipped away. Ben leaned back on the rod and the fish was on. It pulled hard, so it was some time before the pike 'hove into view'. By now Ben was well away from the bank (trying to avoid being pulled in) so I told him to wind in a bit and come to look at the fish. As he peered over the edge of the bank and saw his quarry his face was a picture. He now played it to a sloping bit of bank where I could lift it out. It was a pound heavier than when I had caught it and still in fine fettle.

Nigel with a nice river pike.

There was no way young Ben could pick the fish up so I took a picture of him touching it before we slipped it back. Ben had another fish at the next pool but it was only 7–8lb. However, this second fish almost gave him a heart attack as it launched itself into the air when it took the bait. What a session!

New Year's Eve

It was a while since I'd been fishing and 'cabin fever' was setting in. Lilian decided to spend an afternoon on her archaeology so, round about mid-day, I rang Nigel to ask whether he fancied a spot of fishing. I was told that he was already on the river so I decided to join him.

I grabbed the bag, the rods and the bait and set off to find my pal. When I arrived, he was using a swim feeder and catching grayling. As I watched he hooked his ninth of the session so I went for the camera. I pressed the buttons but nothing happened. Flat batteries? By the time I'd switched batteries the fish was back in the water, so no picture. Nigel's next fish wriggled from his grasp and swam away before I could immortalize it on my memory card – not my day for photography!

After a while with no more bites (I missed a couple), I suggested that we tried for pike. We packed up the gear, returned to the cars and drove to another stretch a couple of miles downstream. I put on a spoon and Nigel used a float-fished dead bait. We had not been fishing long when I had a pull in the middle of a swift-flowing shallow stretch. To be honest, we both thought it might be a salmon but next cast I hooked the fish and it turned out to be a modest pike.

There was no more action for a while and it was beginning to get distinctly gloomy when we got to the last decent pool on the stretch. Nigel's float had hardly settled when there was a swirl close to it – obviously a pike. He cast again and a few minutes later the fish had another go – and again it missed the bait. Knowing that there was a fish interested, Nigel persisted and it must have been ten minutes before the float sailed away. After a fair tussle, the fish was landed and we were able to weigh it on Nigel's new digital balance (a Christmas present from his wife) – 9¼lb. As he pointed out – his 'biggest of the season so far'. We thought that there might be another fish in the pool, so out went another bait. After five minutes the cork submerged again. This fish was obviously bigger and it was quite a while before Nigel was able to net and land it. The fish weighed 28½ lb, Nigel's best yet. What a way to finish off the year!

Poor Fishing

My first fishing trips in 2005 were to the river. We seem to have had nothing but rain and wind lately, so the Frome was up and down every other day. I tried maggot fishing and caught a few dace and a salmon kelt from a tiny side channel, then I went down the main river and landed a couple of pike – nothing special but pleasant enough.

While I was dace fishing, I noticed a splash in the shallows just downstream of a small bridge. When I went to investigate I saw a salmon cutting a redd in the gravel. There were two or three males in attendance, but it was difficult to see them because of the ripple on the water.

A few days later I went out to try for some more dace. The water was still pretty coloured and there had been a frost in the morning, but I was hopeful. I scattered a few loose maggots into the water and began to fish. Having missed the first few bites, I struck too hard and a well-hooked minnow flew back over my head. The next fish was a small dace and then a grayling just a bit bigger. Then the float snapped. I did not have another float with me so I switched to a simple paternoster (the same weight and hook that I had used on my float). By watching for the line to twitch, I could see the bites and I caught dace and grayling just as fast as I could on the float. In fact by striking on every retrieve I had several that I did not know were there. Hopefully, I'll do a bit more fishing before my holiday in early February.

A Cold Day

My friend Peter Lyne came down one Saturday for a spot of grayling fishing and I said that I would meet him at the river. As it turned out I was there first and it was a *very* cold morning with a biting wind from the north blowing across the open meadows. I was dressed for the occasion with three or four layers of fleece, a woolly hat, chest waders and gloves but the blast as I opened the car door was enough to put me off float fishing.

I decided that the best way to keep warm was to do a bit of spinning, so I tied my big spoon on the rod and set off for the river. I found the water with a slight tinge of colour but certainly not enough to spoil my chances with the pike. I thought that with it being very cold my best bet was to work the spoon very slowly, sink and draw, so as to give the pike a chance to strike before the lure disappeared into the distance.

I drew a blank in the first large pool so I crossed over to the far bank and cast about three yards into the opposite slack. As the spoon came flashing back there was a streak of green and it was in the mouth of a pike. I think that the fish was also feeling the cold because it took hardly any line and was soon on the bank, unhooked and returned. Very encouraging! I walked downstream to the next big pool – nothing! Then at

Nigel's twenty-eight-pounder – not the best picture, but one hell of a fish.

Pike caught on a Bulldawg lure. Note that the treble has been removed.

the next one (another 100 yards further down) I had a second take and the fish was well hooked – a bit smaller than the last one. Not much of a fight but as I prepared to slide it ashore the hook came out and it dropped back. It saved me the trouble of another cold unhooking job.

As I looked up I saw Peter approaching across the field, so I walked over to say hello and to have a chat. I watched as he set up and began to float fish, then I fished on for another half hour – nothing else. Anyway, it was a pleasant sunny, if cold, morning and just the way to prepare for my holiday.

I then nipped out for an hour the following Monday afternoon to try out a rubber (Bulldog type) lure recommended (and given to me) by my friend Terry Weldon. I have to say it proved to be very effective, with a long, eel-like tail that wriggled nicely, even on a slow retrieve. I landed three fish and lost one. The lure weighs about 50g and fishes nicely, even in still water. My only doubt is the extra treble under the lure (I took it off); I'm sure it would be fine with only the integral single hook.

Back to the Cold

Back from my holiday in Tobago and the 30°C plus temperatures to a week of freezing arctic winds – brrrrrr! At last I steeled myself for a spot of fishing. I decided to try spinning for pike in the local river and to give the rubber lure (sans treble hook) another go.

I waited until midday to give the weak winter sun a chance to up the temperature from freezing. To be honest, I was not too hopeful because I always think that, in this cold weather, the pike may be reluctant to move for a lure unless it is put right on their nose. After all, why should they expend energy unless there is a *certain* reward. The first thing I saw was a group of wonderful scarlet cup fungi; even in the cold I could not resist a picture.

Sure enough for half an hour I struggled. The lure wiggled nicely through three or four excellent pools, but there was no response. I was beginning to lose interest (and to lose the feeling in my fingers) when suddenly a fish of about 8lb nipped out from under the bank and

grabbed the lure. I was so surprised that I forgot to react and the pike let go again. It showed no further interest despite me spending a whole five minutes on it.

Encouraged, I fished on for a little while before crossing over to the south bank. I retrieved the lure through the largest pool on the stretch and just as it came past a little peninsula of reeds, a pike grabbed it and this time was hooked. The fish put up a spirited show for such cold conditions. It was nicely hooked round the maxilla and when I took hold of the hook it just dropped out.

I fished on for a further ten minutes then, as my stomach began to rumble, I packed in and went home.

Different Rivers

I tend to spend quite a few winter sessions spinning for pike in my two local rivers. Both provide excellent sport and produce lots of fish – in fact, I commented to my friend Nigel that I probably average about one pike every half hour of lure fishing. Of course, there are the odd blanks and equally unusual, hectic sessions but overall the fishing is pretty consistent.

Live and dead baits will generally produce bigger fish than lures – on the whole – but if I stick to *big* spoons, *big* plugs or (as recently) *big* rubber lures, I land a fair proportion of doubles. That is to say, I do from the smaller of the two rivers. In the other, although it contains lots of pike and they do grow big (the biggest pike I have ever seen took a smaller fish that my son Richard was playing on that river) fish in the teens of pounds are much less common. Why?

The answer may lie in the nature of the habitat and the availability of suitable food. However the graphs taken from the same rivers show that growth rate of young fish is similar in both. Perhaps there is not enough decent sized prey to keep the larger pike growing well?

A Fish at Last!

I'd been having 'one of those spells'. For weeks, it seemed, I'd been unable to catch much at all. To restore my confidence (and my sanity) I decided to have a go for pike and/or sea trout in my local river. Now to be fair conditions were not ideal. It was the middle of a hot, sunny afternoon and the river was very low. I considered which lure to use and settled on my old standby a J11F Rapala. Perhaps it's not the best sea trout or pike lure in the world but over the years I've caught plenty of decent fish on J11s. To be absolutely frank, I rarely if ever use lures with more than one treble for pike these days; it's too easy for them to swallow the lot. Anyway, as it was, I knew that there would be lots of weed growth and often the water would be too shallow for anything that dived deeper. I wanted to fish over the weed beds even in the shallow riffles as well as having a chance to stir a fish from the deeper pools. Rightly or wrongly that was my decision.

I began by working my way upstream casting up, down and across in each fishable spot and retrieving appropriately to keep the lure working and weed-free. After about ten minutes I flicked the plug to the far bank in a shallow spot with masses of *Ranunculus*. At the first turn of the reel, there was a mighty crash and a splash and I found myself playing a pike. I bullied it through the weeds and eventually realized that, with the water so low, I was going to have difficulty landing it (no net). I drew the pike into the margin and lay on the bank (a bit unstable and precarious) to try and reach the fish. With a stretch I was just able to get the forceps to the hooks and shake the fish off – what a relief!

Shortly afterwards a fish (it must have been a trout) bow-waved after the lure as I reeled it through the shallow, weedy tail of a pool. It would not take. Half an hour later I was fishing through a deep, dark pool when there was a flash of green and silver and I was into a slightly smaller pike. This one I landed and unhooked without much trouble. Then a bit further on I felt a pluck as the lure traversed two metres of water in mid-river, I glimpsed the shadowy silvery shape of a salmon as the fish turned but it would not come again. As I was about to pack in, a small pike slashed at the lure but was not hooked. All in all a pleasant afternoon and a good confidence-booster.

What Is It?

Mysteries are not unusual in fishing. A little puzzle once cropped up after I had taken grandson Ben fishing a couple of times. It was easily solved, as it happened, but for a short while it had me confused.

Ben was not due to go back to school until Thursday. As a result his mam and dad asked if I could look after him for a couple of days. I never mind these duties with Ben because it always gives me an excuse (as if I needed one) to go fishing. The only problem was that we had to go out in the daytime. The weather was warm and sunny and the tides were not much good for going to the sea. Ben has become a bit disillusioned with carp fishing (like his Grandad, he's not much of a sit-and-wait person). On the first day we decided to go pike fishing in the river. We started off with a big rubber lure and fished for about an hour. The water was low and clear and there was no sign of fish anywhere. We dredged up lots of weed and got stung by nettles and prickled by thistles but the fishing was slow. We had almost had enough but as we walked back to the car Ben suggested that I changed the lure. I tied on a big, silver spoon and after five minutes fishing, just as I retrieved past a large island of floating watercress, we saw a pike come out and follow the spoon. The fish grabbed the lure and I handed the rod to Ben – what a tussle! It rushed all over the river and eventually, just as we were wondering how to land the pike, it buried itself in a dense weed bed and managed to extract the hook. The pike had been about 10lb and we were both chuffed with the excitement.

The following day Ben wanted to try for pike again, this time with wobbled natural baits. We started off by using a grayling (that I'd found dead) on a single circle hook. First cast Ben had a take and a fish of similar size to the one that escaped the day before seized the bait. Ben played it manfully for a few minutes, but eventually it let go (it was never on the hook). We fished a few more spots to no avail, then we returned to the place where the first pike had been lost. This time it was a couple of minutes before it took and it was well hooked in the jaw. Ben played it to a standstill and we managed to take a picture.

Then came the mystery. When I downloaded the pictures there was a ghostly, grey irregular shape on the left-hand side. I couldn't imagine what it might be. A bit of investigation revealed three or four mackerel scales stuck to the lens of the camera. I flicked them off and the problem was solved, but the pictures of Ben's nice pike were not improved.

Caught! (But Only on Camera)

When I got down to the river the other day, it was low, very low. The water was clear and the weeds were dying back so there should (I thought) be no problem spinning. However, for some reason there was lots of weed drifting downstream. Nothing too big, but countless little bits of *Ranunculus* – just enough to foul the lure and stop it working almost every cast.

I tied on a J9 plug and fished for a while, hoping for a sea trout but, apart from one brownie of about 1lb that grabbed it in the shallows, splashed clear of the water and came off, nothing! Time was pressing on, so I decided to have half an hour with a pike lure. I fastened on the long, rubber lure that caught me some good pike last season and walked along casting into what I thought were likely places. The lure fished and wriggled along nicely but for a while there was no sign of life. In fact I was just about to pack in when I decided to have a 'last cast' into a deep slow pool. As the lure trundled along in the depths, still clearly visible, there was a flash of green and I found myself hooked into a moderate pike.

After the problems I had reaching fish without a net last time I tried fishing, I had clipped my small net to the bag on my back using the artery forceps (I hate lugging nets about when I'm fishing). Anyway, I decided to take a picture of the fish on my line before I netted it. The pike (only 5–6lb) was decidedly lively and for a minute or two it kept surging away and gradually it picked up a sizable clump of drifting weed. By holding the rod in one hand and the camera in the other I was eventually able to get a picture. I slipped the camera into my pocket and stooped to pick up the net. As I did so, the line went slack and the pike swam away – that's

the problem with trying to get pictures of fish in the water!

Talking about pike, I had a recent email from a friend, Chris Harrison. Chris had been watching a pike from a bridge. The fish swam in under some weeds and, following a bit of a commotion, swam out again chomping (a fish?). The curious thing was that when the fish emerged it had 'lit up' to almost a lime green colour. Now I know that marlin and some other tropical predators light up with glowing colours when they are feeding but I've never heard of pike doing it. I'd be interested to hear from anyone who's seen this in pike.

Piking Again

The rivers had been so awful recently that I had not even considered going fishing. Of course it's a seasonal thing. Throughout the spring and summer months, water plants grow in profusion and act as a trap for sediment. Mud and sand accumulate in thousands of tonnes on the river bed in the low summer flows. The autumn rains, usually about this time of year (October), raise the water levels, speed up the flow and shift the flow patterns with the result that much of the accumulated sediment is disturbed. This sequence of events is why the 'first floods of autumn' are generally very dirty. The water in my local river – usually sparkling clear – has recently been like thick cocoa.

Anyway, I was becoming a bit frustrated with the constant dirty water. Twice I had driven to the river only to find it totally unfishable. To cut a long story short, it was with mixed feelings that I went the other day to find it looking like weak tea with only a dash of milk. Far from ideal for pike spinning, but I felt that I was in with a chance. I was using my bass spinning gear so removed the plug and tied on a large silver spoon thinking that it would maximize the visibility of the lure in the turbid water.

As I approached the river, I walked alongside a narrow ditch in which the water was gin clear. I thought that it might just hold a pike sheltering from the flow so I walked to the edge to have a cast. As I did so, a jack shot away at my approach – encouraging! I fished all the way to where the ditch met the main river to no avail. Obviously the fish I had scared was the only one in the ditch. Just outside the mouth of the ditch was a shallow weedy bay and second cast a green torpedo lunged out of the murk and grabbed the lure – success! I played, landed and returned the pike. By now I was really optimistic, but it was misplaced. For the next half hour I spun assiduously without even a sniff of a pike. In fact there were not all that many 'pikey' places to fish and I must have walked the best part of a mile while I was fishing. I was just thinking about 'giving them best' when I reached a fairly deep stretch (about a metre or so) with a slow flow along my bank. I made several casts straight downstream and retrieved parallel to the bankside. Suddenly there was a splash and a flash just under my stance and the second pike of the session hooked itself. A satisfying spell of fishing for such unpromising conditions.

Of course it is possible that pike, having undergone a period of enforced fasting when the water is dirty, feed well as it clears and they can once again see their prey. Similarly, after a long dark night the first light of dawn could be a prime time for action.

Semi-circle Pike

I'd been itching to try out some semi-circle hooks for pike fishing. For a couple of seasons I had been using circle hooks with good results and I expect that they will remain my standard approach until something better comes along. However, there were some Varivas semi-circles (that I was given) in my bag and I wondered whether they might be just as good as the full circles for bait fishing. At this time of year pike are the obvious species to try them out on so I did.

I tackled up with half a wine-bottle cork for a float, a semi-circle on some 20lb wire and my usual 'bass' rod and reel. The first place I tried, I had a bite and after playing the fish for a while it came unstuck – I guessed that it was 7–8lb from the occasional glimpses. Anyway, the pike refused to take another bait so I moved on. Things were a bit slow and it was half an hour before I had another bite. This time the fish slashed at the bait as I was lifting it from the

water and missed it completely, so I was confident that it would have another go. Sure enough a couple of minutes later away went the float. I waited for five seconds and then gently raised the rod to tighten the line. At first the fish seemed uncertain what had happened then it tore away. The pike was soon landed, unhooked (perfectly nicked in the jaw) and released. It was another twenty minutes and two pools later before I had another bite – at the end of a ditch. This time I played the fish into the ditch where it was again landed – once more perfectly hooked.

I decided that, to finish off the session, I'd have a go for the one that I had lost at the start. It was a couple of minutes before the float shot under (about a metre from where it had taken the first time) but it was not to be caught. It pulled hard for about ten seconds before coming free. I decided that it must be something to do with the fish – I've met these 'Houdini' pike before – and the way it gripped the bait. It certainly felt as though it was hooked both times but presumably it was just clamped down tight on its meal!

Christmas is Coming

I haven't been fishing with Nigel for a long time. After returning from a holiday in Belize, I gave him a ring to see what had been happening on the local fishing front and it seemed it had been a bit quiet. Anyway, I asked if he fancied a spot of coarse/pike fishing the following afternoon and he jumped at the chance. The following morning when I got up, the ground was white with frost – not auspicious. I was glad that we had decided to meet at about mid-day to give things a chance to warm up a bit.

I arrived about five minutes before Nigel and by the time he drove up I'd already had several nice dace. He took his float rod out of the car and immediately began where I'd left off, catching dace after dace. After a while we decided to give the dace a rest and go piking – this was when I had the surprise. Nigel produced his pike rod and instead of the usual float it was adorned with a golden Christmas bauble. Apparently it was a reject from the tree and rather than waste it, he had turned it into a festive float.

We'd scarcely cast out our baits before I heard the word 'pike' and saw Nigel's rod well bent into a fish with the golden globe ducking and diving into the river behind it. After a bit of a scrap it was landed and returned. We fished on for a while with no result then it was announced that the fancy float had decided to fill up with water so it was replaced with a more normal version. In the next couple of hours we had four more pike (Nigel three, me one), all but one (the last) of a decent size and all nicely hooked in the corner of the mouth.

After writing my last freshwater web page I had a query about whether my 'semi-circle' pike were foul hooked (the hook looked as if it was outside the mouth). I said that I thought not, but promised to look next time out. In fact, as I suspected, the hook was simply in the soft tissue under the maxilla (upper lip) of the fish and had pulled up behind it, making it look as if it was above the mouth – so no problem there.

Festive Fishing

My grandson Ben came over to stay armed with his Christmas hat, rod and tackle box so I knew that we had to go fishing. By some miracle there was no frost on the appointed morning so I felt that we were in with a chance. I donned my own festive headgear and we set off.

Ben was quite keen to try one of the local lakes, but I persuaded him that the river would be a better bet. I had a few maggots left from a previous trip so we decided to try and catch some bait then to have a go for a pike.

It turned out that Ben had left his floats at home, so I dug out an old porcupine quill and we set up his 'dace' gear. When we reached our chosen fishing spot, I threw in a few maggots and Ben began to trot his float down. It was only a minute or two before he began to get bites and before long he had landed a couple of nice dace. 'You have a go while I have a sandwich,' he said. So I picked up the float gear. Of course, my first dace was minute and I suffered all the usual mockery regarding my ability to catch decent fish (he's just eight, but they soon learn don't they?).

Shortly afterwards I saved face by catching a grayling, then a couple more respectable dace. By now Ben had eaten his sandwiches and biscuits so we packed in and set up the pike rod. Now I wouldn't say that he is impatient but I doubt that the float had been in the water for more than a couple of minutes before he was asking why he hadn't had a bite yet. I counselled patience and he quietened down. Fortunately, it was only a couple of minutes more before there was a boil and away went the cork. Ben was using one of the semi-circle hooks that I'm trying out and he tightened into the fish nicely. It struggled hard but he played it sensibly and I was able (at risk of a ducking) to slide it ashore – 8–9lb – very nice! Unfortunately, the hook was in the back of the throat (I don't think this would easily happen with a full circle hook), but I managed to remove it with no damage to the fish.

We moved on to another swim and in went Ben's gear again. This time the water was only about two feet deep so we set the float at about half the depth. The bait drifted round for a couple of minutes and then, as if by magic, a long green shape appeared behind it. The pike hardly needed to move to engulf the bait and Ben was into his second fish. This one, neatly hooked in the lip, was more of a problem and it was a good five minutes before we managed to bank it. Just over 20lb – his second twenty.

Young Ben into his second twenty-pounder – is he pleased?

When I think how many years it took me to land a 20lb fish it makes you wonder. He's obviously got the equivalent of green fingers (fish fingers?). I can't wait to take him again. Oh! That won't be for a while, his Dad's just rung to say that he's broken his arm. Merry Christmas, Ben!

The First Fish of the New Year

I met Nigel down by the millstream at twelve o'clock. It was an amazingly mild day for the time of year, a bit of cloud cover but essentially bright and sunny. We began by trotting maggots in the flow and it was only minutes before we were catching nice dace. After landing a number of fish, we went down to the main river to try for pike.

Both of us were using similar gear – our 'bass' spinning rods and reels with small floats and hooks on short wire traces. The main difference was that I still had on a semi-circle hook while Nigel used a full circle. Our baits had scarcely been in the water for ten seconds when my float zipped under. I raised the rod and found myself attached to a nice pike. After a spirited battle, Nigel did the honours with the net and I was able to return a fish of about 12lb.

Shortly afterwards and a little further upstream, Nigel had a take from a smaller pike but it was not hooked and unusually, refused to have another go. I crossed over the river and after a while had another pike a bit smaller than the first – then it went quiet. We fished a couple of really 'pikey' pools to no avail. Not a sniff of a pike. Then we moved down to the lowest pool and began to fish simultaneously. Nigel's float was the first to disappear and after a while I netted a near double for him. I returned to my own rod and within a couple of minutes the float submerged with a loud pop. The pike was nicely hooked and Nigel again helped with the net. I'd scarcely returned it when my pal had another bite and landed the same pike that he had put back ten minutes earlier.

That was the last pike of the day. We spent half an hour trotting for grayling – nothing! I put on a plug and had a go for pike but apart from a couple of knocks (trout or salmon I think) there was nothing doing. Anyway, it was an excellent start to the year – lots of dace and four different pike landed. I can't wait to go again.

No Pictures

Just occasionally things go wrong. I went fishing one afternoon, hoping to catch dace and grayling and to finish off with an hour's pike fishing. It turned out to be a lovely afternoon with temperatures of about 9° and with my first cast the maggot was taken by a cracking dace. I grabbed the camera and switched it on, focused it and pressed the shutter release (or whatever passes for a shutter release in digital cameras) – nothing! I looked at the screen and in bold red letters were the words CARD ERROR. I took out the card and put it back in – CARD ERROR. I took out the card and wiped it – CARD ERROR. I blew into the works, fiddled with the batteries and switched it on again – CARD ERROR. By now I was getting the message – the card was dead.

I resigned myself to not getting any pictures for the website and fished on. I had a wonderful afternoon. Almost every cast produced a good dace and after I had fed maggots in for half an hour, the grayling began to feed and I landed several nice fish around the 1lb mark. When I tired of catching fish on the float gear, I went after pike and first chuck landed a beautiful twelve-pounder that was soon followed by five more – nothing massive but all nice fish. I was well pleased with the session and but for the camera problem I'd have had some excellent pictures.

The following day I went into Poole and bought a new card.

Same Fish, Different Method

At last the camera is fixed and I have some pictures. These things are never as simple as they seem. In this case I bought a new card for the camera and Jessops only had a 256 megapixel (much larger capacity) version in stock. It worked fine in the camera so I went fishing and took some pictures of the pike that I caught. Then came the problem. When I tried to download the pictures – nothing! I fiddled with the little card reader, fiddled with the computer, fiddled with the camera – still nothing! As chance would have it I had just, that morning, had an email from my friend Ben Lagden. Having read of my flash card plight on the website, Ben had offered future help if I needed it (he's an IT expert). I rang him and to cut a long story short he came over, took the camera and card away, downloaded my pictures, got me a new reader and told me that my old reader was incompatible with the new larger card. Would you believe it?

Anyway, enough of that. As I said, I took my spinning rod to the river armed with my 'Bulldawg'. It was a lovely afternoon, quite mild and windless. I worked my way through a few pools without a sniff just enjoying being out on the bank at last. After twenty minutes or so, I got to the pool where my grandson had caught his twenty-pounder (on bait) a couple of weeks back. I cast across and retrieved a couple of times, then the third cast was along the slack water. Half way back I could see the lure wiggling slowly towards me when – wallop! It was grabbed by a big fish that surged away and, in the shallow water, crashed and splashed about alarmingly. Eventually it was subdued and I was able to land it.

It only slightly took the gloss off the catch when I noticed that it was the same fish that young Ben had caught before. Still, at least it was caught using quite different tactics and was the biggest pike I've had on either that rod or that particular lure up to now.

A Different Approach to Piking

I enjoy spinning! I make no apologies for my addiction but having said that, I know that using artificials is not always (or indeed often) the best way to catch big fish. However, some years ago when I regularly fished with my pal (then also my research student) Stuart Clough, we developed an approach to pike fishing that I'd almost forgotten.

In essence we tended to use live or dead baits for our pike, knowing that there was a good chance of double-figure fish or better in the water that we fished. We both liked to spin as

well and sometimes we would have a spinning session just to see what we could find. It was quickly apparent that when we were spinning we covered much more water and sometimes caught pike from the most unlikely spots; places that we would never even have tried with the natural baits. We then evolved a strategy in which one of us used a big spoon or plug (we alternated who was spinning between sessions) and the other used the 'naturals'. If a fish had a go at the lure and missed, the 'spinner' called up his buddy and ninety-nine per cent of the time the pike took the fish bait within seconds of casting out. This was certainly our most productive tactic and gave us many good fishing sessions.

To be honest I'd almost forgotten about our 'dual method' approach until I went fishing yesterday. I met my pals Nigel and Ben down by the river. It was a lovely afternoon and by the time they arrived I'd already caught sufficient baits for them to fish. They opted to spend a bit of time float fishing before we started and caught a reasonable number of dace, roach and gudgeon on maggots.

I didn't see much point in three of us using natural baits, and to be honest I wanted my pals to catch a few fish, so I opted to use the rubber lure that had been successful for me last week. I thought that perhaps I could find a few fish that we might not otherwise have located. Both Nigel and Ben were using simple float gear with short wire traces armed with single circle hooks. I did not fish at first, being keen to get a few pictures for the website, and in the first pool they came across a pike of perhaps 6lb that just didn't want to be hooked. To be fair, Ben was not familiar with the use of circle hooks and probably mistimed and overreacted on the first couple of occasions that the fish grabbed his bait. Anyway, we decided to give that fish best and walked on downstream.

As we walked on, I hung back behind the others and had a few casts with my lure. On probably the sixth or seventh cast a decent fish grabbed at the lure and was not hooked so I called to Nigel, who was fifty yards ahead of me by now, to come back and have a go. Within a minute or two he was into a cracking fifteen-pounder, which we landed and returned after taking a few pictures.

'Big Ben (Lagden)'s'
twenty-five-pounder – he
soon got the hang of not
striking with the circle
hooks.

Shortly after Nigel's fish, Ben had a smaller one, which he landed on his own at the expense of getting himself bogged down in the muddy margins. We walked on a bit further and I cast across to the far bank and picked up the smallest pike so far (4–5lb) on the lure. Two or three casts later there was a swirl, right under my feet, as I lifted the wiggling rubber from the water. I called for my nearest mate, this time it was Ben, and within seconds he was into the fish. This one fought like hell and it was only when Nigel netted it that we realized it was a real beauty. The pike was in mint condition and weighed over 25½lb.

Shortly after his big fish, Ben hooked and lost another fish that I ultimately landed on the lure. All in all it was a wonderful afternoon. Of course it's possible that I would have landed either or both of the larger pike on my lure, had I persisted. However, by switching to natural bait they were almost guaranteed and of course because we were using circle hooks both were lightly hooked in the jaw and returned absolutely none the worse. Fantastic!

Why Don't They Bite?

Pike generally seem fairly easy to tempt in my local rivers. However, there are days when even the most promising spots appear to be devoid of fish. Now when I'm fishing in the sea it's easy to make the excuse that the fish aren't there but in the river there *must* be fish in at least some of the spots. So why don't they bite? There will, of course, be times when the water temperature is too low or too high for the fish to be active, but if you catch one or two fish that's hardly likely to be the case. A similar argument can be made for when the water is very dirty, etc. If one pike will bite, why won't the others? It must surely be something to do with the differing states of hunger of the individual fish.

On my last two trips we had a couple of examples of fish that wouldn't bite. In the first instance I was fishing with my pal Steve Pitts. We had an excellent afternoon catching half-a-dozen pike on natural baits. Near the end of the session we were fishing a large and very 'pikey' looking pool. After about twenty minutes we had searched most of the likely spots and were thinking about moving on when suddenly Steve let out a gasp. I asked what was the matter and he said that the biggest pike he had ever seen had just swept past his float-fished bait without touching it. Encouraged and knowing that if you find a pike it will often take, we both fished for a further twenty minutes in the area where he had seen the big fish. Despite our best efforts, there was no sign of the pike. The conditions were clearly OK because we caught a number of nice pike between 6–15lb, so why was the big one so reluctant to take?

Steve Pitts – into a pike.

Getting down to it – Steve's pike makes a powerful run.

A couple of days later I went with Nigel for another afternoon's piking. Again we used natural baits, some float-fished and some wobbled. Of course we tried 'Steve's spot' again – to no avail. In all we landed twelve pike this time – an excellent session you might think. However, after we had already caught eight or nine fish, I was wobbling my dead dace through a deepish pool when it was taken by a pike of perhaps 8lb. We landed the fish and released it then I continued fishing just a metre or two from where I had caught it. As I watched my bait lurching along about a metre beneath the surface, a massive green shape appeared from beneath the marginal weeds and slid past the flashing bait without touching it. Encouraged, we both tried hard to tempt the big fish (incidentally not the same fish that Steve had seen two days earlier – the pool was miles away). No success except that only a few metres from where I had seen the big pike I caught another of about 4lb – much the smallest of the trip.

Why didn't they bite? These were two fish that we actually knew were close to the baits but after the initial lunges they showed no further interest. Of course, it makes you think that on many other occasions there must be pike close to your baits that just ignore them.

One event during the second trip may have thrown some light on the matter. Nigel had been drifting his bait past a very likely looking spot under a raft of floating vegetation. He said afterwards that the bait had passed within thirty or forty centimetres of the weed on perhaps five occasions with no sign of life. Not knowing this, I dropped my bait in the same spot and allowed it to swim right in under the raft. The weeds heaved and I was into a pike. Now this fish seemingly couldn't be bothered to move even half a body-length to take a bait, but when it was literally 'on its nose' it grabbed it. Even though we caught lots of pike, it was a pretty cold afternoon following a hard frost so the water temperature was certainly low.

The following day I was talking to my son Richard on the phone and I mentioned the reluctant pike. His comment was that our baits probably weren't big enough. Now whether this is true or not, there is no doubt that pike (and other fish) have a built-in 'cost/benefit' assessment mechanism. There are a number of things that control the amount of effort that they put into catching a meal. For a start if they have not eaten for some time and their bellies are empty they will be much keener to feed. Consequently a very hungry pike will attack more persistently and from a greater distance than a well-fed one. Similarly, if it's cold the fish may be sluggish and less inclined to move very far to take a bait. Finally, if there is a danger of being eaten or attacked by a predator (fish, bird or possibly human), they will be less likely to expose themselves to risk by feeding.

In short, if you want to catch a big, well-fed, scared pike you will be wise to keep well out of sight and put a big, slow-moving, attractive bait right on its nose and that's what we'll be trying to do later this week.

Tired of Pike?

To be fair, although pike are beautiful animals, they are not the greatest battling fish in the world. Often they make the reel scream a few times in the course of being landed and sometimes they crash at the surface or even leap, head shaking violently, from the water but they rarely look like escaping from my bass gear. However, there is one aspect of piking that really *is* enjoyable and that is 'the take'. I tend to use three methods when I'm after pike and they all produce fantastic takes. Firstly I spin with big spoons or rubber lures. Secondly, I wobble dead fish hooked on a circle hook through the snout. Lastly (and I have to say my favourite and most effective), I fish a live fish under a slit wine-bottle cork float (easily slipped onto or off the line if necessary).

The rivers I fish are usually shallow and clear, so that whichever tactic is in use I often see the fish take. This is the best bit. The lure wobbles along slowly swinging from side to side or wagging its tail. I guide it close to the edge of weed beds or rafts of floating vegetation drifting in slack pools of water. Suddenly my heart leaps as a green flash hurtles after the metal spoon – amazing! Wobbling dead fish provides similar heart-stopping action but because the bait is almost neutrally buoyant I can easily swim it along very slowly, let it sink into river bed depressions or twitch it to make it shudder or dart past a known lie. When I float-fish with live bait, the cork glides along on the surface. Sometimes the bait drags it under, but if it does its jerky response to the short wave flapping of the bait tells me that there is no pike. Like all float fishing, it's easy to concentrate on what you are doing because there is always something to look at (the cork) and you need to steer it gently into the most likely spots. Sometimes I see the pike swirl after the bait, sometimes the cork goes under with a loud plopping sound and sometimes it simply submerges at a steady pace. Always it takes my breath away for a few seconds.

Anyway, to return to reality. Last time I mentioned a couple of big pike that wouldn't take our baits. I also mentioned that my son Richard had commented that my baits probably weren't big enough! Yesterday I went for a spot of dace fishing. I had a brand new barbless hook and some new shot, having inextricably tangled my rig in brambles on the last trip. I began to fish and within a few minutes had landed three

stonking dace – the best one probably 6oz. Remembering what Rich had said about a big bait, I thought I'd try for the big pike so I put the float gear away, picked up my pike tackle and set off downstream (bass rod, Stradic reel and 4/0 circle hook on a short wire trace). I only intended to try two spots – both where we had seen big pike. At the first one, my bait was taken within about two minutes of it being swung into the water. I saw the fish take and it was about 12–15lb. It swam round for a few seconds and then came off, having removed the bait. It refused to have another go but I was not too bothered because it was not the fish I was after.

I moved on to the other pool where Steve had previously seen the 'monster' pike. For fifteen minutes the bait (my biggest) wandered around unscathed. I was beginning to think that there was nothing doing again. I walked round the edge of the pool, trying every likely looking patch of weed, bay and raft of debris – nothing! I'd been trying for about half an hour (almost unheard of for me to fish one pool for so long) and decided to give the 'hot spot' one last go before 'giving them best'. I lowered the bait

31lb of river pike. The pike was electro-fished later that winter – still in fine condition.

Steve Hill with an excellent pike caught on livebait from the Dorset Frome.

into the water and waited. As I looked down at the reel I noticed a little tangle (my first for years believe it or not) in the braid up near the butt ring. Obviously I had been careless with the slack line as I moved my bait from place to place. Instead of doing the right thing and lifting my bait from the water until I untangled the little knot, I tucked the rod butt under my arm and began to pick it out with my fingernails. As I picked at the loops suddenly the line began to tighten in my fingers – horror of horrors, a fish had taken the bait!

For a second or two my brain was numb (number than usual). What should I do? No chance of getting the knot out now and it would

be a tragic weakness in the line. I decided to wind the little tangle back onto the spool and hope that I could coax the fish ashore without subjecting the tangle to any pressure. Fortunately my ruse worked. By gently easing the fish along under my rod tip I managed to keep the problem firmly on the spool and eventually to land the fish. Phew! Thirty-one pounds of pike!

Fishing Pals

The last time I fished with both my pals Steve Pitts and Steve Hill was a couple of years ago in Tobago. This time it was a bit different – colder for a start. We'd arranged to have a day's piking on my local river. In fact the story started a couple of weeks earlier when we had organized a similar trip. On that occasion Steve Hill was ill and did not turn up so the other Steve and I had to catch the pike without him. This time he was not to be put off and they both turned up at about eleven o'clock having driven down from Bristol. After a quick cuppa to revive them we were off to the river. Conditions looked good – low and clear – and it did not take long to catch a few baits. It was cold – but not too cold – and we were really optimistic.

We started off using three different tactics. Steve Pitts was using a fly (I thought it looked more like a feather duster than a pike lure), the other Steve put on a live bait and I wobbled a dead bait. It was only a few minutes before I had a take over a shallow mud bank. The fish was fairly small (5–6lb) but it was encouraging to get one so soon. After that it was fairly slow. Despite fishing a couple of nice pools, none of us had a sniff for perhaps twenty minutes. By now both Steves were using live baits. It's hard to remember the exact sequence of events but we landed two or three modest fish. The best was perhaps a nine-pounder that took my dead bait as I dangled it right under the hanging branches of a willow tree.

We ate our lunch on the move and after walking a mile or so down river and covering all the best looking spots we decided to try another stretch for the last hour or so. Before we returned to the car to make our short trip to the other reach we decided to try one last pool. Pittsy picked up his fly rod again but Steve Hill remained faithful to the live bait. He was right! Only minutes after he had cast out the float slowly submerged. At first it looked as if the bait was dragging it under but it stayed down and as he tightened it was clear that it was a decent pike. After a few seconds of play the fish let go so Steve dropped his bait in again. Sure enough it was soon taken and this time there was no mistake – the circle hook was nicely in the edge of the mouth. After a fairly lively struggle Steve landed a beautiful fifteen-pounder.

We packed in and moved to the other stretch where we landed two more pike making our total eight fish for the day. Very satisfying!

Not Much Fishing

It had been one of those weeks. Firstly, a series of things to do at home then visits to Bournemouth, London, Littlehampton and Salisbury, then some really rotten (if much needed) wet weather – all of which curtailed the fishing and the web page production. I did manage one day at the river almost a week ago. It was sunny, cold and clear and the water was very low after the long dry spell. I decided to try a Mepps in the hope of catching a decent perch. I used a size 3, thinking (but not convinced) that it might avoid the smallest fish if there were any about.

As it turned out, the perch were on strike and I never saw a single stripe or red fin all afternoon. However, it occurred to me that the braided line has changed things for the better when it comes to using fast spinning lures such as Mepps. In years gone by I would have used a couple of swivels, one at the head of the lure and another up the trace. Even then there would have been a fair chance of the nylon monofilament springing into a nasty tangle due to line twist. Nowadays, using my nice soft braid, line twist seems to be a thing of the past. At least it no longer causes problems. Of course I had a single small swivel in the set up in order to attach the short wire anti-pike trace but I think that even this was superfluous. I'm sure that the braid accumulates lots of twists in the course of fishing but it does not result in tangles. Amazing!

Anyway, to return to the fishing. I'd not been at it for more than five minutes when I had a firm pull and hooked a fish. The sun was bright and due to reflections off the water it was while before I got a view of my catch – the brain was thinking 'big perch' but when it hove into view it turned out to be a smallish pike (I should have guessed I suppose). I plodded on downstream

Nigel Bevis landing a fine river pike for our pal Ben Lagden.

and it must have been almost a kilometre before I had another bite – a second pike – it looked as if the perch were really on strike (or technically 'off strike' I suppose).

A while later I came to a fast shallow stretch. There was a small slack behind a tree on the far bank that looked like a possible spot for a perch or pike. I flicked the Mepps up and across and began to retrieve. The current dragged my line round and as the lure swept into the fast water I felt a yank – missed it! I tried again and this time saw a big silver flash in mid-river – missed again! Third cast I hooked a fish, which splashed about as I wound in – an out of season trout. I released it and decided that this was probably a good spot to try when the trout fishing starts in April. There's always something to be learned even on a poor day.

Localized Pike

Over the years I've often read of big catches of pike from small areas of a lake or river.

Of course, the words 'aggregation' and 'pike' sound like a contradiction. It is well known that pike will behave as cannibals and that in some waters one of the main foods of big pike is their smaller relatives. The River Frome near my home is no different to any other river in this regard and small pike are quite often found in the guts of big pike. As it happens small pike are not very good live baits – they tend to sit in one spot and so do not 'search the water' for something that might eat them. They are much better when used as wobbled dead baits but perhaps no more attractive than a dead dace or a mackerel 'flapper'.

Anyway, the point is that you wouldn't normally expect to find more than one pike in a particular 'lie' or ambush point. In fact radio tracking has shown that at times a couple of similar-sized pike will lurk within metres or even centimetres of each other. However, in late winter it seems not uncommon for considerable numbers of pike to gather in a single pool and I had an example this week.

I was fishing with Nigel and I was using dead

baits (from my freezer) hooked through both lips on a size 4/0 circle hook. The biggest bait I had was perhaps 20cm in length. I was fishing with my usual spinning rod and it was easy to lob the bait across the river if I needed to. My second cast into a deepish pool (perhaps 2m deep) was down and across. As I twitched it past a small mat of floating plant debris under my bank, a decent pike shot out from under the cover and grabbed it. I played the fish for a couple of minutes and Nigel was just picking up the net to give me a hand when the fish came unstuck. I had another cast to the spot where the fish had let go and sure enough it took again. This time we landed the pike – a nice fifteen-pounder.

The fish was returned and my next cast brought the bait (the same bait) sliding past the mat of rubbish again. Out swept a pike and grabbed the fish. This one was firmly hooked and landed – 8–9lb. I commented to my pal that the pike seemed to have come from exactly the same place as the first one. After a few more casts we had no further bites and thinking that the pike were 'mad on' we wandered off upstream. Half an hour and one small pike later we returned, this time on the opposite bank to the one that produced my first two pike. To cut a long story short, within the next ten minutes or so we landed four more (different) pike including a cracking fish of 22lb from more or less opposite the first 'hot spot'.

We moved on downstream but a further hour's fishing failed to produce another bite, despite some of the places looking 'perfect'. What do we deduce from these events? Well for sure there were at least six pike ranging from 4–20lb in a single pool no more than ten metres wide by twenty metres long. A couple of kilometres of river upstream and downstream of the productive pool seemed pretty barren. We used the same tactics throughout the session and fished the best spots we could find. It seems that, on this occasion, the pike were concentrated in one small area. Clearly they were actively feeding and the biggest fish we caught was certainly capable of devouring the smallest one. Presumably this is some sort of aggregation related to the forthcoming spawning season. The moral? Obviously, even after catching a

fish, it's always worth another cast or two to the same area.

The Pike's Revenge

There are obviously lots of big pike about at this time of the year (pre-close season). Of course, they don't appear by magic and they were in the river over the past twelve months but, whatever the reasons, more of them are caught in February and March just before the season's end. My last website piece on 'localized pike' stimulated a fair bit of email and, not surprisingly perhaps, several other anglers reported exactly the same phenomenon of several decent pike holed up in a small area while the rest of the river appeared to be devoid of life. Obviously it's well worth searching for these hotspots rather than plonking yourself down in one place and waiting for the pike to find you.

Anyway, as I say there have been several good catches recently. My pal Richard gave a good example (different river to me). Here's his email, slightly edited:

Hi Mike
It was good to see you the other week [we'd met by accident when we were both fishing the same stretch] *and I managed just one small jack on the last cast just above the bridge with not even a follow on the rest of the river.*

Anyway have just read your latest piece on pike gathering together and thought I would tell you of the same experience on Saturday. I was fishing wobbled roach again and worked my way up from the Bridge trying several good-looking swims without even a follow. I came to a deep run just above a bend where I had two fish this time last year on a spinnerbait tight in to the near bank. This time I took a nice fish of about 8lb and one of 3lb again tight to the bank and then nothing else so moved on.

I covered the water all the way up to the concrete bank without the slightest sign of a fish so decided to sit out the last hour float ledgering where I had taken the two fish. I trotted the roach about ten yards down the near side and let it come to rest about two feet from the bank. In just a few minutes there was a tap on the line and the float moved out into mid-river and I struck into a large fish.

The fish bottomed my 22lb scales and is my first twenty, not a pretty fish and not a good photo but I was over the moon. Again, strange how all the fish came from one swim with nothing showing anywhere else on the river.

All the best

Richard

Another pal, Stuart Clough, reported a similar good catch (a third river) and wondered whether the fish might be concentrated downstream of an obstruction such as a weir pool or some shallows. However, I think we need a lot more evidence before we can decide. Clearly it would be really useful if it was possible to predict the whereabouts of such pike concentrations.

On a slightly different slant another friend, Guy, sent me a picture of a cracking forty-inch fish (23lb?) taken on a fly while salmon fishing last week.

My own exploits were less impressive, but perhaps more amusing. I decided to have a 'last afternoon wobble' with a few frozen baits. I was using a 4/0 circle hook nicked through the snout (both lips) of the bait. My first fish (about double figures) took on the first cast. I'd left the net behind so it was a bit of a palaver leaning down the bank to unhook it with the forceps – beautifully hooked round the maxilla.

Five minutes later I hooked another fish (slightly smaller) under the roots of a huge willow tree. I knew at once that I had a problem. I was well over a metre above the water standing on the concrete wall above a weir. Immediately upstream of me was a metal bridge. The fish was well-behaved and I led it into the shallow water on the concrete apron of the weir. I would have to cross to the upstream side of the bridge, climb over a fence and drop down the wall to get at the fish and unhook it. I poked the rod tip under the bridge and laid it down on the ground so that I would be able to get hold of it after crossing the bridge. Then I nipped across and began to climb over the fence. At this point the pike decided to go back into the river and I saw the rod begin to bend alarmingly. I panicked and in trying to get back to save the rod my foot slipped off the rail of the fence. My full weight dropped onto the top bar of the fence, crushing two very tender parts of my anatomy. For an instant I was speechless, then I just groaned – it was agony. I staggered back and picked up the rod – miraculously the fish was still attached.

Try again, Mike! This time, after leading the pike into the shallows, I took the bale arm off – at least it wouldn't pull the rod in. I crossed the bridge, scaled the fence again (rather gingerly) and dropped down onto the weir. Needless to say, the fish had swum off again so I began to handline it back towards me. After a couple of minutes of give and take I had it by my feet. I took the hook in the forceps and twisted. The pike thrashed, the forceps slipped the line caught on the concrete and snapped just above the trace. I looked down to see the pike, motionless and gently finning, just below me. Rolling up my sleeve I reached down and took its tail fin (all I could reach) between my finger and thumb. I slowly manipulated the fish until I could shift my grip to just behind its head. A quick lift and I was able to lay it on the wet concrete. I removed the hook (again nicely round the maxilla) and slipped the pike back into the water. It swam away and I picked up my gear and limped home. Next time I must remember the net.

FURTHER READING

Basic Accounts

Easily readable accounts of the natural history of pike, or of pike angling, can be found in:

Maitland, P.S., and Campbell, R.N. *Freshwater Fishes of the British Isles* (Harper Collins, London, 1992)

Pye, D. *The Way I Fish* (E.M. Art & Publishing Ltd, Peterborough, 1964)

Scientific Research

More scientific (jargon-heavy!) pike books are:

Craig, J.F. *Pike, Biology and Exploitation* (Chapman & Hall, London, 1996)

Linneaeus, 1758, *FAO Fisheries Synopsis No. 30, Rev. 2* (Fisheries and Agriculture Organization of the United Nations)

Raat, A.J.P. Synopsis of biological data on the northern pike *Esox lucius* (1988)

Journals and Conference Proceedings

Much of our own work on pike, and that of our friends at the Centre for Ecology and Hydrology, has been published in scientific journals and conference proceedings. These include:

Beaumont W.R.C., Cresswell B., Hodder K.H., Masters J.E.G., Welton J.S. (2002) A simple activity monitoring radio tag for fish, *Hydrobiologia*, **483** (1–3), 219–224

Beaumont W.R.C., Masters J.E.G. (2003) Management and Ecological Note: A method for the external attachment of miniature radio tags to pike *Esox lucius*. *Fisheries Management and Ecology*, **10** (6): 407–409

Beaumont W.R.C., Hodder K.H., Masters J.E.G., Scott L.J., Welton J.S. (2005) Activity patterns in pike (*Esox lucius*) as determined by motion-sensing telemetry in: *Aquatic telemetry. Advances and applications. Proceedings of the fifth Conference on Fish Telemetry held in Europe, Ustica, Italy, 9–13 June 2003. pp. 231–243.* Rome: Fisheries

and Agriculture Organization of the United Nations

Hodder K.H., Masters J.E.G., Beaumont W.R.C., Gozlan R.E., Pinder A.C., Knight C.M., Kenward R.E. (2007) Techniques for evaluating the spatial behaviour of river-fish, *Hydrobiologia*, **582** (1), 257–269

Masters J.E.G., Welton J.S., Beaumont W.R.C., Hodder K.H., Pinder A.C., Gozlan R.E., Ladle M. (2002) Habitat utilisation by pike *Esox lucius* L. during winter floods in a southern English chalk river. *Hydrobiologia*, **483** (1–3): 185–191

Masters J.E.G., Hodder K.H., Beaumont W.R.C., Gozlan R.E., Pinder A.C., Kenward R.E., Welton J.S. (2005) Spatial behaviour of pike *Esox lucius* L. in the River Frome, UK. In: *Aquatic telemetry. Advances and applications. Proceedings of the fifth Conference on Fish Telemetry held in Europe, Ustica, Italy, 9–13 June 2003. pp. 179–190*

Volume **601** of the journal *Hydrobiologia* (2008) contains the proceedings of the American Fisheries Society's International Pike Symposium, full of papers on pike biology.

Other Scientific Papers

These used to be difficult to find outside of University libraries, but many of these journals can now be found online.

Bregazzi, P.R. & Kennedy, C.R. (1980). The biology of pike, *Esox lucius* L., in a southern eutrophic lake. *Journal of Fish Biology* 17, 91–12.

Burkholder, A. & Bernard, D.R. (1994). Movements and distribution of radio-tagged northern pike in Minto Flats. In: *Fishery Manuscript.* pp48 Anchorage: Alaska Department of Fish and Game

Chapman, C.A. & Mackay, W.C. (1984). Versatility in habitat use by a top aquatic predator, *Esox lucius* L. *Journal of Fish Biology* 25, 109–15

Cook, M.F. & Bergerson, E.P. (1988). Movements, habitat selection and activity periods of northern pike in Eleven Mile Reservoir, Colorado. *Transactions of the American Fisheries Society* 117, 495–02.

Diana, J.S. (1980). Diel activity pattern and swimming speeds of northern pike (*Esox lucius*) in Lac Ste. Anne, Alberta. *Canadian Journal of Fisheries and Aquatic Sciences* 37, 1454–1458

Helfman, G.S. (1981). The advantage to fishes of hovering in the shade. *Copeia* **1981** (2): 392–400

Jepsen, N., Beck, S., Skov, C., Koed, A. (2001). Behaviour of pike (*Esox lucius* L.) >50cm in a turbid reservoir and in a Clearwater lake. *Ecology of Freshwater Fish* 10, 26–34

Kipling, C. & Le Cren, E. D. (1984). Mark-recapture experiments on fish in Windermere, 1943–1982. *Journal of Fish Biology* 24, 395–414

Lucas, M.C., Priede, I.G., Armstrong, J.D., Gindy, A.N.Z., De Vera, L. (1991). Direct measurement of metabolism, activity and feeding behaviour of pike, *Esox lucius* L., in the wild, by use of heart rate telemetry. *Journal of Fish Biology* 39, 325–345

Mann, R. H. K. (1976). Observations on the age, growth, reproduction and food of the pike *Esox lucius* (L.) in two rivers in southern England. *Journal of Fish Biology* 8, 179–197

Mann, R. H. K. (1980). The numbers and production of pike (*Esox lucius*) in two Dorset rivers. *Journal of Animal Ecology* 49, 889–915

Mann, R.H.K. (1982). The annual food consumption and prey preferences of pike (*Esox lucius*) in the River Frome, Dorset. *Journal of Animal Ecology* 51, 81–95.

Nilsson, P., Anders & Brönmark, C. (1999). Foraging among cannibals and kleptoparasites: effects of prey size on pike behaviour. *Behavioral Ecology* 10, 557–566.

Ovideo, M. & Philippart, J.C. (2005) Long range seasonal movements of northern pike (*Esox lucius* L.) in the barbel zone of the River Ourthe (River Meuse basin, Belgium). In: *Aquatic telemetry. Advances and applications. Proceedings of the fifth Conference on Fish Telemetry held in Europe, Ustica, Italy, 9–13 June 2003. pp. 191–202.* Rome: Fisheries and Agriculture Organization of the United Nations.

INDEX